TLÖN:
JOURNEY TO
A UTOPIAN CIVILISATION

AuthorHouse™ UK Ltd.
1663 Liberty Drive
Bloomington, IN 47403 USA
www.authorhouse.co.uk
Phone: 0800.197.4150

Published by AuthorHouse 07/14/2015

ISBN: 978-1-5049-4098-6 (sc)
ISBN: 978-1-5049-4099-3 (e)

authorHOUSE®

TLÖN : JOURNEY TO A UTOPIAN CIVILISATION

Aristidis G. Romanos

in memory of Elina

TABLE OF CONTENTS

1. THE STORY OF THE MANUSCRIPT

Two significant and, no doubt, inter-related events prompted me to write this paper: one was the reading of a short story by Borges entitled "Tlön, Uqbar, Orbis Tertius"[1]; the other was the acquisition, in an auction sale, of a unique and unknown manuscript of Lithuanian origin, dating from 1408. Borges writes about a benevolent secret society in the early 17th century which undertook to invent a country. *"At the end of some years of conventicles and premature syntheses, they realized that a single generation was not long enough in which to define a country"*[2]. Their work was passed on from one generation to the next, through a system of electing devoted disciples, who in turn became master/scholars. The involvement in the secret brotherhood of the ascetic millionaire, Ezra Buckley in Memphis, Tennessee, in 1824, meant an enormous boost for the project. He found too modest the scheme of inventing a country, proposed instead the invention of a planet and suggested a systematic encyclopaedia of that planet, backed by his millions. *"About 1944, a reporter from the Nashville, Tennessee 'American', uncovered in a Memphis library, the forty volumes of the First Encyclopaedia of Tlön"*[3]. In them a complete history of the unknown planet appeared *"with its architecture and its playing cards, its mythological terrors and the sound of its dialects, its emperors and its oceans, its minerals, its birds, and its fishes, its algebra and its fire, its theological and metaphysical arguments, all clearly stated, coherent, without any apparent dogmatic intention or parodic undertone"*[4].

Before my fascination from reading Borges's brilliant account of the fictitious planet had faded from my mind, a copy of the 15th century Lithuanian manuscript happened to come into my possession. I leafed through its thick pages trying to decipher its content by its magnificent illustrations -for, I must admit, my knowledge of Lithuanian is very limited- and, as I did so repeatedly, I was more and more intrigued by the feeling that I was holding something particularly valuable. The manuscript is an architectural sketchbook and diary kept by Ladislas, an obscure Lithuanian[5] exile living in Holland, who, during the last part of the 14th and the beginning of the 15th century had visited the site of a legendary country and a long-disappeared civilisation.

4

Images of unknown buildings set in beautiful landscapes and mythical city plans, others drawn in black ink and others painted with phantasmagorical colours of turquoise, emerald and purple, filled its pages. Unfortunately many of them as well as many of the text pages had been damaged by fire. As I learned subsequently, the manuscript had belonged to a private collection which was partly destroyed during the great Covent Garden fire of 1868.

The description of the ruins of that lost civilisation and the occasional reference in the diary both to a local mythological tradition and to previous written sources bear an uncanny resemblance to the 'fictitious' country of Tlön described by Borges; so much so that I began to wonder whether Borges may not have been aware of the evidence in favour of the existence of that civilisation and may not have moulded Tlön on the lines suggested by Ladislas in his travel diary. To have pretended that Tlön is a creation of human imagination is, I feel, very much like Borges's sense of humour.

The excitement from the anticipation of the possibility that Tlön was real prompted me to study both texts, take notes of their similarities and dissimilarities and arrive at a first rough consensus.

The extraordinary fact was that the manuscript remained in obscurity for about five hundred years until it passed, sometime in the middle of the 19th century, to the possession of Leonid Krk, one of the leading rare book collectors in London. Krk, a notable scholar in Baltic literature, who translated the manuscript into English, was later sentenced for fraud; most of his possessions and his Drury Lane residence, or what remained of it after the 1868 fire, were confiscated. The manuscript was sold at an auction to Caspar Amorson, a Scandinavian urban planner, known for his passionate interest in architectural utopias and his self-financed research in their history, an activity that brought him to the verge of bankruptcy. At that point Caspar, a longtime friend of mine, offered to sell the manuscript to me. I reluctantly accepted, mainly as a gesture of sympathy and help towards the restoration of his state of finances. It was only through my subsequent perusal of the document, that I was aware of its great value and that my interest in utopian literature was instigated.

The gratitude which I then expressed to Caspar Amorson was doubled when he later donated to me a counterpart to the manuscript: a copy of Krk's text, translated in English and annotated by Caspar; with a wealth of comments and explanatory remarks made during the time of his repeated readings of the manuscript.

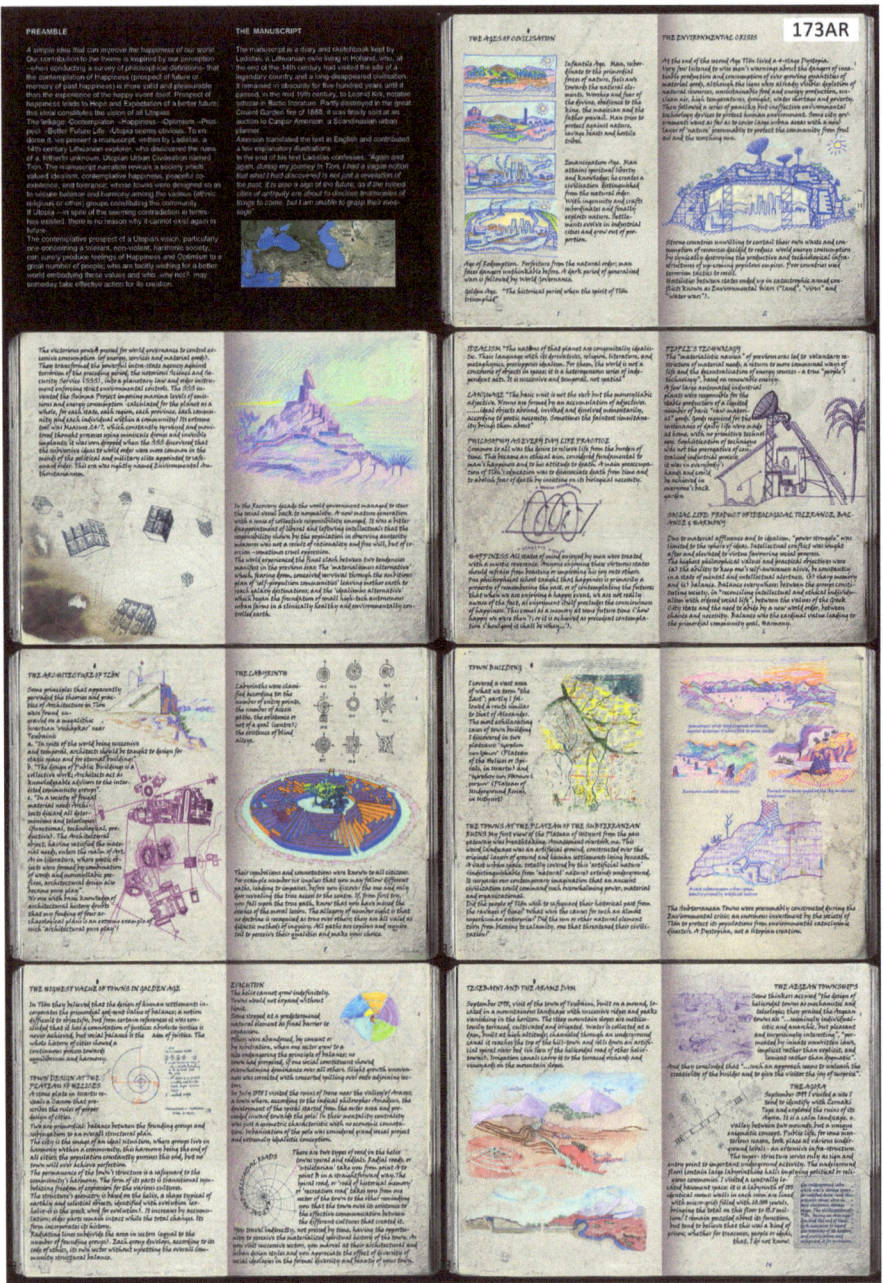

Pages from the Ladislas Manuscript

Caspar Amorson's elaboration of the manuscript functions both as a mediator in understanding or deciphering many issues that would otherwise have remained obscure and also as an imaginative restaurateur and vehicle of futurology; Amorson puts forward his own speculative interpretations of certain events or periods of Tlön's historical past as showing the path to the future of our turbulent present. It is not of course known to many that Amorson, in his short and low-key intellectual career, has repeatedly flirted with the idea of Endless Recurrence, the notion that history advances in repetitive circles, as in fact Borges did[6].

So Ladislas describes things of the past and Amorson comments on this description from the additional distance and accumulated knowledge of about seven hundred years. Sometimes his incisive remarks confirm to me the rather alarming fact that the narrative of Tlön's ages of civilisation bears a remarkable resemblance to some traits and experiences of contemporary life and to certain hypotheses about our world's future. However my doubt remains whether the history of our civilisation is in fact following a repetition of cycles or whether the past eras of Tlön as described by Ladislas were just prejudiced by the terrors of his tortured imagination and were formulated by a deliberate choice to portray his fears about the future as factual events of a distant past. To this neither Caspar Amorson nor I are able to give an undisputable answer, but it is worth noting that Ladislas, somewhere towards the end of his text confesses: *"For me this journey is not just like any other reconnaissance or archaeological expedition. Again and again I felt a dramatic uneasiness and had a vaguely perplexing notion that what I had discovered in my expedition is not just a revelation of a past civilisation, it is somehow also a sign of the future; as if the ruined cities of antiquity are about to disclose testimonies of things to come, but I am unable to grasp their message"*.

In this essay, beside my references to Ladislas's original text of the Lithuanian manuscript, as translated by L. Krk, I unavoidably also refer to the extensive commentary of Caspar Amorson, which makes the content more directly relevant to the contemporary reader. My work consists in codifying the narrative about Tlön in a few thematic chapters; the structure is totally different from that of both Ladislas's diary as well as Amorson's commentary, but I tried to remain faithful to the spirit and content of the original text and present, at the same time, Amorson's relevant observations.

The involvement of Borges in the subject of this essay deserves an explanation: the fact that there are remarkable coincidences between the fictional Utopia (as in Borges) with the factual description of the ruins of a historical past, even though distant (as in Ladislas), convinced me and Caspar Amorson (with whom we perused, comparatively examined the two texts and had vehement arguments on the subject) that the two texts refer to the same unique urban culture, but seen from different viewpoints. Since Ladislas does not, surprisingly, give a name to his ruined civilisation[7], I shall refer to the Utopian country as Tlön throughout the text. The similarities between the two utopias lead unavoidably to the probability that Borges may have been aware of the Lithuanian manuscript, which he deviously –and legitimately- used as a basis to build his masterly plot about the imaginary planet of Tlön. Maybe the Argentinian's shrewd judgment led him to suspect that Ladislas's journeys may have also been fictional!

This coincidence explains also the seemingly self-contradictory idea of my essay putting implicitly forward my hypothesis that as Utopia had existed, it can therefore be also decoded, perhaps even reconstructed by Utopian Archaeology. However, I am making a plea for assistance and co-operation to anyone who, in the course of one's diatribe with the study of the history of civilisation or the history of town planning and architecture, has come across any source of information about that distant past, or had some sudden revelation or inspiration about it, or -which is less likely- is so old as to remember it. I am doing this in the belief that, together, we can at least complete the puzzle of the salvaged pages and replace the ones missing from the sketchbook -if we cannot conjecture the incomplete content of the philosophically biased diary.

So let me first describe in outline Tlön's history of civilization, philosophical theories and beliefs, its way of life, and its social organisation before going on to the material manifestations of its culture, such as architecture and town building.

The four Ages of
Civilisation of Tlön
as described by
Ladislas

sketch C. Amorson

2. THE FOUR AGES OF CIVILISATION

The Ages of Civilisation of Tlön are described, in a laconic and pictorial way, by Ladislas, in the first Chapter of his Diary. Amorson produced one of his best sketches to illustrate in a diagrammatic way the Ages of Tlön following the same structure with Ladislas, but slightly altering his nomenclature to make it more readily recognisable to our contemporary experience: the Infantile Age, the Emancipation Age and the Redemption Age.

Ladislas writes:

"From a tabernacle probably used as a teaching device I transcribe a description of aphoristic style and brevity, written in some Hellenic dialect, about the first three ages of civilisation and make copies of the ideographs carved on it. I have never come across such a bold and in some aspects even subversive text. Besides, there are statements and terms that I find difficult to explain or to interpret, such as «οικολογικός» and «βιωσιμότης»[8]. For instance no explanation is given about the nature of the deposition from natural order (was it a moral one?) nor about the causes of the "generalised wars"; it is only hinted that humanity was somehow becoming too greedy in producing (and also in cosuming) more than was really needed. Here is how the text reads:

<u>The Infantile Age of Humanity</u> Man, subordinate to the primordial forces of nature, feels awe towards the natural elements. Worship and fear of the divine, obedience to the king, the magician and the father prevail. Primitive technical tools assure life's continuation and basic protection against natural disasters, savage beasts and hostile tribes. The exorcism of fear and need reigns. The settlement is the place of physical security from the enmity of natural phenomena, whereas the countryside represents the domain of fear, insecurity and exploration. A stereotype authoritarian ideology and a paternalistic religion emerge enabling the control of men's beastly instincts, the appeasement of their alarming fears and the survival of the race.

The Emancipation Age of Humanity Man liberates himself from the bondage of the supernatural and attains spiritual freedom. By a constant pursuit of knowledge and technical progress man creates a human civilisation quite distinguished from the natural order. With technical ingenuity and crafts[9] and science as spearheads man subordinates, utilises and finally exploits nature. Settlements evolve in cities dedicated to industrious production and cities grow out of proportion. The house is individualised and becomes a home, the private oasis offering retreat from the desert of city life; gradually the city turns into a space of social threats. Man seeks security and calmness in the countryside. An overwhelming trust in the triumph of science and crafts led to the adoption of a cynical rationale of material "overproduction and overconsumption". Anything imaginable was possible and humanity felt too powerful to be able to use its power wisely.

The Age of Redemption The world enters its third period, a period of forfeiture from the natural order, and faces dangers unthinkable before. A dark period of generalised wars follows. The emerging victorious states establish a global power which promotes a single authoritarian ideology intolerant to all others and pursuits the establishment of a world order".

A fourth one, named Golden Age, holds a special place in the document, as it represents and describes what Ladislas, and every reader of his Diary, identifies with *"the historical period when the spirit of Tlön triumphed"*. Its birth can be virtually traced to the time of the outburst of the exceptional phenomena that marked the history of Tlön towards the end of the second Age and those of the following Redemption Age.

The Crisis

It seems that about the end of the second Age the civilisation of Tlön went through a very serious crisis. The environment of the earth was becoming more and more hostile to the human race, as if nature was taking revenge for the latter's conceit to treat it as an inexhaustible resource to be tamed and exploited while all ecological systems were being driven to breaking point.

Amorson, -who seems particularly interested in this rather minute in terms of historical time but crucial era- has done an extensive investigation of Ladislas references on the matter. He writes that the crisis took only five decades to culminate, as it can be presumed that the phenomena that caused it grew at an accelerating pace. In this short period of time Tlön witnessed a dramatic effort to rehabilitate the overturned state of balance between natural phenomena and human activities of the past age. It went through successive states of inertia, of panic, of abortive technological reforms, of high tensions and of serious collisions. The general state of uncertainty ended up in the establishment of an oppressive, even cruel, world regime which managed to reinstate *"natural and social order"* but at the cost of the suppression of civil liberties and personal freedom. Amorson identifies this period of Tlön's history with an environmental crisis, similar to the one facing our world, for which he coined the term Environmental Authoritarianism, and, through research and comparative analysis of other sources, distinguishes three periods in its development and resolution.

First Period. This was distinguished by the indifference to wise men's agonising warnings about the dangers of the insatiable appetite of humanity to produce and consume ever growing quantities of material goods, when the signs were already visible. "Depletion of natural resources, growing incapacity of mother earth to sustain food production at the required levels, shortage of energy, on one hand, and unclean air threatening health , high temperatures, drought, water shortage on the other are forcibly constructing a new inhuman nature and a new unnatural humanity"[10] In this period a minority of philosopher/rulers, united in a peaceful confederation, tried to persuade, by word or deed, the powerful rulers (as well as those aiming to become such), the democratic communities of the world and the great mass of people to take measures in order to avert more disasters. The movement took two forms: preachers were preaching the need for changing the way of life and practicing abstention and voluntary moderation of material consumption. At the same time an entire armour of what amounts to environmental technology innovations, devices and reforms was put to the service of communities aiming to create a protective umbrella to human environment. Some city governments went as far as to invest enormous amounts in covering large areas of their city with a new layer of 'nature' to protect it from the calamitous effects of scorching sunlight alternating with freezing storms and to allow filtering of foul air.

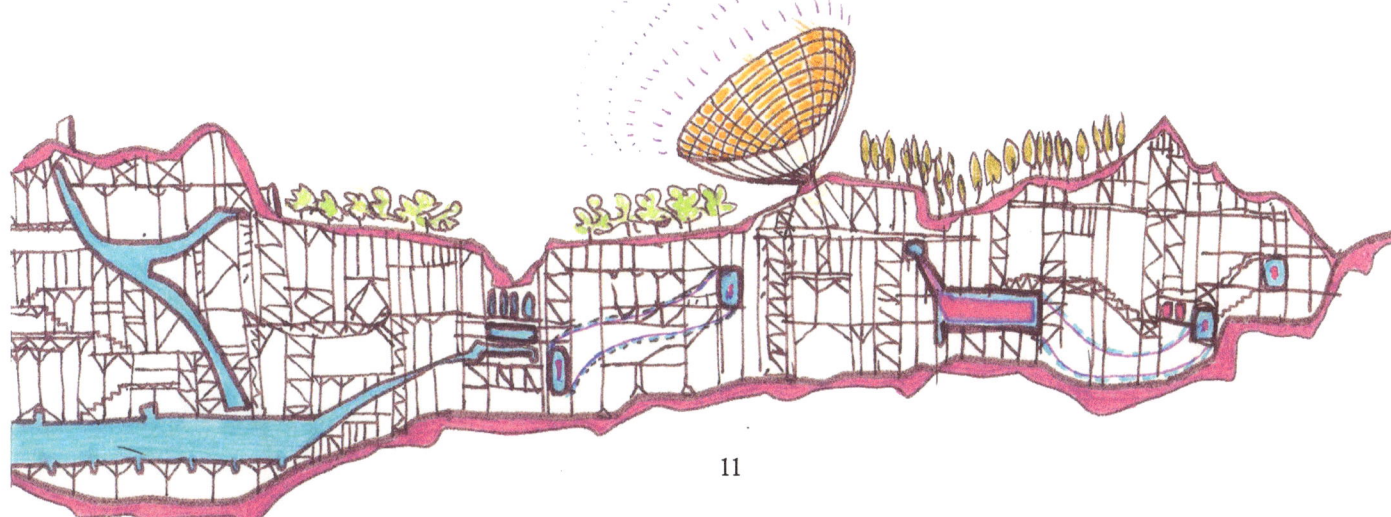

At least one orthodox creed took an unexpected step and –in an effort to adapt its morality to the realities of the ecological crisis- transformed its forgiveness dogma from "turning the other cheek"[11] to "if your neighbour makes abuse of consumption, do not be tempted, but increase your abstention". In the same spirit the practice of fourty days fasting preceding the greatest religious festivity was extended to include, apart from nutrition, the consumption of high-energy products and services. But such efforts, which aimed at changing the way of life and the world economy through a voluntary accession to a New Faith, remained ineffective, as the ideology of materialism proved insidiously luring. The world was seemingly not ready –or not able- to adopt willingly an ecological behaviour.

Second Period. Then followed a long period of destructive hostilities between states of city federations at the end of which the winners exerted pressure for establishing a powerful instrument of world governance. The period started with catastrophic armed conflicts known as *"land wars[12]", "virus wars"* and *"water wars"*. At some point the powerful states passed onto what would in present times be termed Cyber Wars, the effort to outdo the enemy's (declared or anticipated) Controlling Brain, equivalent to a communications network that monitored and managed all technological infrastructure; but this weapon was soon abandoned, as the special intelligence units spying and destroying opponent soft and hardware were so efficient that the ping-pong speed of surpassing each other reached a pace that rendered the whole thing impractical and costly. So the powerful states reverted to the A B C weapons of earlier times (atomic, biological and chemical).

Land wars were of two types: *desperation wars* resulting from the migration of starving populations in the extended torrid zones of the earth condemned to lasting drought; and *aggressive wars* instigated by states, that, incapable or unwilling to curtail consumption of resources and waste in their own territories and after exhausting what we recognise today as their right of purchasing pollutants, attempted to reduce the levels of world energy consumption by cynically destroying the productive, educational and technological infrastructures of up-coming empires with massive populations. The world reverted to a state of a New Dark Age.

The reader must have noticed that Amorson gives a particular emphasis on the relevance of this era to our present state of world affairs and tends to be carried away and transcribe Ladislas's descriptions using a contemporary vocabulary. As this is the result of his comprehensive delving into a rather specialised subject and his synthesis of facts and references found disorganised and scattered in the Lithuanian manuscript –a lot of them rendered incomprehensible or inscrutable by fire- I am reverting to his notes and quote him for the rest of this chapter.

"One is truly astonished by the advanced level of technology that some nations or city states seem to have reached, if one translates in contemporary terms the devious sophisticated engineering and biological devices they used to cause artificially what were perceived as natural disasters by indigenous populations. Virus wars were the most "conventional" weapon of massive extermination promoted by SSS, the powerful Science and Security Service, the first sinister instrument in the service of the allied powerful nations. One of SSS's renowned heads, Shamus Al Zarghaid, is known for having said: "virus wars are an efficient and hence legitimate mode of world population control".

Water wars took the form of contaminating water reservoirs and purification plants of enemy metropolitan areas; this was in essence a type of virus war, but enriched with biological genetically active substances with long-term destructive consequences extending over many generations.

Water wars resembled the earlier era wars for the seizure of areas rich in mineral deposits (mainly oil) and gas, then the primary sources of energy production. During this era nations engaged in fighting to secure water sources. All important hydrological basins of the globe became the objects of fierce conflicts using sophisticated weapons and engineering technology.

This was an era of international anomy, when local wars were breaking up constantly and any perversely cruel means of destruction were considered legitimate: strong states relied on sheer military force, poorer ones used terrorism tactics".

Caspar Amorson comments with bitter sarcasm at the fact that what finally emerged as a most efficient instrument of planetary law and order –with environmental control as one of its main objectives- was, ironically, an offspring of the war against blind terrorism, a phenomenon that had in previous decades plagued a large part of the world. This was a plan known as Summa Project, a transformation of a world-wide Big Brother machinery set up by SSS as a shield against the alarmingly escalating terrorist acts by fundamentalist groups, used by marginal states in the previous era.

Amorson carries on: "Anti-terrorism measures culminated in the creation of an on-line information system, powerful enough to monitor individuals' activities and behaviour, supported by a network of special commando units empowered with authorities of policing, controlling and forcibly intervening if necessary. As a consequence, personal rights and liberties were curtailed to a degree surpassing Orwell's or Huxley's imaginations, in particular free movement, free gathering and free speech. Originally controls went as far as attempting to impose 24/7 surveillance "by miniscule drones and invisible implants"[13] that would monitor thinking processes - having absolute access to people's brains. But soon this intention was dropped -and hushed up- as it was found during the trial period that the most subversive ideas to world order originated not in the minds of the underdogs or the "wretched of the earth"[14] -as was assumed- but in those of the political and military elite appointed to safeguard and protect it. The moral was that once a controlling mechanism of such power is established as a legitimate and necessary measure for combating social evil, enormous pressures by economic and political forces build-up to maintain the mechanism long after the evil is banished".

Amorson notes with interest that, in spite of the mechanism's sophistication, terrorism was not abolished by anti-terrorist security measures. The efficiency of the system did not neutralise the desperation of 'human bombs', so that terrorism tended to be always one step ahead of anti-terrorism.

"It took years of fanaticism,[15] narrow-mindedness, reciprocal fear, obscurantism and abundant bloodshed of innocents (at the end of the second era the world population had shrunk to about 60% compared to its level at the end of the first era) before intelligent minorities within the societies of world powers convinced the latter to drop the manichaeistic[16] notion of "the axis of evil" (propounded by powerful lobbies) and decide to have an insight not only in the way terrorists act, but primarily in what were the deeper causes of the phenomenon that was termed terrorism and why it was generated basically among people from oil-producing countries. Understanding the real problem was half the solution; the rest followed almost in a natural order, until a peaceful settlement addressed to these causes and based on justice was finally agreed, but this was only possible in the third era, when a strong central government was established to lead the world out of the crisis.

Third Period. The delayed-reaction of the world community to the ecological crisis marked the dawn of the third period. After many futile efforts to beat black technology with green technology (similar to contemporary measures such as the switch of developed nations' source of energy production from oil to Renewable Energy and the prevalence of fuel-cell engines in automotion) and to create a new ecological morality to which the peoples of the earth would voluntarily adapt, a world-wide omni-present and omni-potent political government was formed by the powers that emerged victorious from the cruelty of the environmental wars; the government imposed on the world the Summa Project. All local governments were convinced, coerced or forced to accept this pact and to subordinate all actions of the state to the strict commandments set by the all-encompassing plan to "heal nature".

The world was finally attempting to design the globe's evolution, but long after it was evident that this was at the brink of total breakdown. It was doing so the hard way by using methods inherited from the fight against terrorism. The Summa Project was run by a technocratic and intellectual elite recruited by the World Government to function as a secret environmental police, whose presence everybody felt, but very few actually witnessed.

This was a Project that originated in the ur-antiquity, but had a taste of a distant (or not so distant) future. It was a force majeure scheme in social planning and engineering; its objective was to implement a series of measures designed to re-establish equilibrium in the planet's environment. Measures involved the abolition of the use of all non-renewable resources and the imposition of maxima levels of emissions and energy consumption. These levels, analytically calculated for the planet as a whole, were then defined as quotas for each state, each region within a state, each province within a region, each community within a province and each individual within a community! Moreover, the plan prescribed, not just for private and public bodies and interest-groups (of an economic, social, cultural, religious or political nature), but to individuals within the body or group as well, exact consumption levels for all goods and services.

Since these levels differed according to the individuals' respective roles in society, the Project calculated model consumption plans for each type of professional role within the societal structure; it then went further and defined numbers of types of jobs per community and finally ended up in drafting a totally planned economy, both from the aspect of production as well as from that of consumption.[17]

Ironically, the world community now slipped in a state of hard-fisted, all-encompassing communism, promoted and finally promulgated by those same nations which had championed total laissez-faire economies over the previous periods of time.

The era of Environmental Authoritarianism

The era of Environmental Authoritarianism was on and populations were treated like subjects rather than like citizens. People's lives were dictated by central forces and virtually predetermined to a large degree. Unconventional behaviour was unthinkable, censorship over spoken or written word prevailed and any criticism of authority was prohibited. The social organisation and institutions set up to enable this subordination of private lives to the pursuit of a common goal surpassed even the wildest dreams of Marxist theoreticians and of communist regimes.

De-escalation of consumption became a crucial notion in everyday life. There was rationing in the consumption of food and beverage, of clothing, of certain important services and, above all, of energy consumption. Every individual's right of recreation travelling was calculated and fixed in number of kilometres per annum. People had to wait for months or years to travel for vacation, once they had exhausted their personal annual quota. This made life much more complicated from what we witness today, as everyone had to exercise sophisticated planning to make the best of limited consumption allowances. The necessity for careful planning in everyday life proved particularly difficult in practice, as it contradicted the idealistic schools' belief in considering time programming as hubris.

The limitation on physical contact, counterbalanced, no doubt, by increasingly cheaper and more effective long-distance communication, had serious implications upon the behaviour and psychology of people and upon the established morality. Private means of physical transport were unthinkable and condemned, except for those propelled by muscular power or renewable energy, with mass transport considered morally superior. Fines for attempting to break the rules and cheat the system were very severe and meant usually the loss of personal liberty for long periods of time.

Public administration was entering new fields of corruption, motivated by influential persons' demands to falsify their data of energy consumption. Favouritism in the form of forged certificates of consumption was the commonest offence among civil servants. On the other side there were often cases of electronic crime when hackers entered official records and faked electronic data of individuals' energy consumption behaviours; when discovered, they were sentenced to life imprisonment.

The population accepted the Summa Project with a variety of attitudes ranging from trust and good will to sheer opposition. Intellectuals as usual split in many currents of thought, which were soon grouped in two main trends: the progressive and the traditional.

At first the progressives -which took the restrictions imposed entirely objectively on a material basis without immediately investing them with idealist implications- prevailed, particularly as the public was under the shock of discovering that the state of the earth's environment was really in danger and not at all a picture painted by fanaticism and doom mongering.

But, as the oppression of restrictions prolonged in time and the young generation was gradually waking up to the realisation that its well-being should literally be sacrificed for the sake of rescuing the planet from ecological break-down, the traditionalists' message (that the methods of total planning and absolute controls adopted by the Project were violently suppressing liberties and humanistic values) began to gain momentum. The population was stirred up into opposing restrictive measures and confronting the regime by open acts of defiance. Some groups adopted methods of passive resistance, such as the No-walls-communities: exasperated by the Big Brother monitoring methods they constructed their dwellings without external walls deliberately exhibiting their private lives to any passer by and to the Surveillance Authorities.

Progressives retorted that the resistance movement was not morally legitimate in view of the real dangers and that it was but a convenient excuse to justify people's inertia to the radical change of the way of life that the urgency of the situation demanded. So the few weak pockets of traditional / humanistic resistance diffidently appearing in various provinces were soon crushed by the oppressive methods (such as psychological terrorism, imprisonments, arrests and solitary confinement of opposition leaders) of the environmental police, directed by SSS, under its notorious leader Jacob Benedictorich Ästlin. The world succumbed to SSS's iron fist. The Summa Project was finally implemented -true, at great cost- but

The reaction of the "no-walls communities"

with visible results as to its environmental targets; the population accepted its inevitability and learned to live under its extreme restrictions and quasi-military rules.

The Recovery Decade

The Summa Project Implementation period lasted for two full decades and was followed by the Recovery Decade, a period in which the world government managed to steer the social vessel back to normality with great care, ingenuity and wisdom, avoiding the reefs and rocks of belated uprisings of guilty consciences who had refrained from rebellion when the pressure was on! But these measures proved to be unnecessary. The people of Tlön rose when they knew that no real issue was anymore at stake; and they rose in a dignified, determined but non-violent unity and crushed the institutions of the world regime without a nose bleeding right at the time that world government itself was about to relinquish power to small communities.

Out of this "unhappy era of self-denial"[18] a new disciplined and mature generation with a strong sense of collective responsibility was emerging. It was almost too good to be true. In fact one of the greatest disappointments of liberal and leftwing ideologies of the age was exactly the bitter acknowledgement that the impressive sense of social responsibility evident in the population as a whole was a result of coercion -sometimes of cruel oppression- and not of rationality and free will. Anexikakos put an end to this -tormenting to the left- issue by arguing that "coercion was only phenomenal and that most people in fact transcended conventional morality by deliberately subordinating the values of personal liberties to a cause that they conceived as being of prime importance to their survival", a position to which the perplexed conscience of the left readily acquiesced. Gradually the people, and in particular the people of developed nations, acquired a new morality of international justice in accepting that they should bear first, as the champions of ruthless development in the previous centuries,

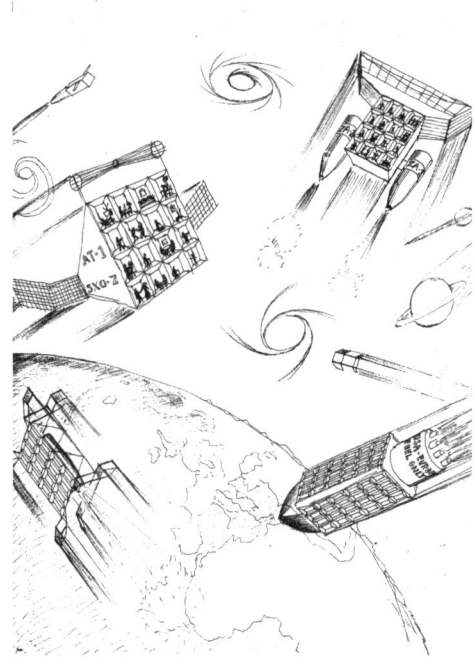

Self–propulsion communities

the cost of the new movement. Some intellectuals branded this attitude as a practical blend of Christian-cum-communist philosophy.

During this Recovery Decade, marking the beginning of the Golden Age, as Amorson was able to document, "occurred the final clash between the two different tendencies manifest within the world community from previous eras. The 'materialismus alternative' which, fearing that the earth was doomed, conceived human survival as an exodus of the human race from mother earth achieved through the ambitious plan of 'self-propulsion communities' which were to reach galaxy destinations; and the 'idealismus alternative' which planned the foundation of small high-tech and high efficiency autonomous urban farms in a clinically healthy and environmentally controlled earth which would allow people to lead a life of bodily and spiritual bloom, exercising in sports, recreation and philosophical and artistic creation". Amorson suggests that this was the utmost in energy and energy sustainability that man ever reached and notes that the clash ended in favour of idealism.

Tlön was living the dawn of its Golden Age.

Landscape of Aegean high-tech
sustainable farms settlement

3. THE GOLDEN AGE

Philosophy and language

The most succinct adjective to describe the mentality of the people of Tlön is *idealistic*. Borges gives an eloquent description. *"The nations of that planet are congenitally idealistic. Their language with its derivatives, religion, literature, and metaphysics, presupposes idealism. For them, the world is not a concourse of objects in space; it is a heterogeneous series of independent acts. It is successive and temporal, not spatial"*[19]. Consequently, in all languages of Tlön, nouns are not in use. In one group of languages the fundamental elements to express any notion of objects or happenings, are *"impersonal verbs qualified by monosyllabic suffixes or prefixes which have the force of adverbs. For example there is no word corresponding to the noun moon, but there is a verb to moon or to moondle."* In the languages of the northern hemisphere *"the basic unit is not the verb but the monosyllabic adjective. Nouns are formed by an accumulation of adjectives. One does not say 'moon'; one says 'airy-clear over dark-round' or 'orange-faint-of-sky' or some other accumulation [......] ideal objects abound, invoked and dissolved momentarily, according to poetic necessity. Sometimes the faintest simultaneity brings them about"*[20]. So objects are formed of two, three or more elements. Using certain abbreviations, the process is practically infinite.

I have insisted on the question of Tlön's language because it is fundamental in understanding many of its cultural manifestations and it exhibits best its prevailing idealist mentality. That mentality permeates all manifestations of life. It is interesting to note that, contrary to what one might expect (that idealism would negate any science), sciences exist, in countless numbers. In some, incidentally, one finds remarkable affinities to contemporary scientific notions, as, for example, that of space-time (*"they do not conceive of the spatial as everlasting in time"*).[21]

Philosophy in Tlön was the main preoccupation of all, thinkers, metaphysicians or laymen, and although idealism was the orthodox doctrine, the attitude that philosophy was a kind of dialectical game, where beautifully constructed systems –based on real, probable or totally imaginary premises- competed with each other in perfection and consistency, allowed the production and the preaching of an abundance of doctrines including opposing and contradictory ones. There was great sensation in Tlön when, during the Age of Great Migrations, certain commercially developed states pressed for a reversion to materialism, propounded as a 'modern' and 'practical' life outlook. A milder attempt at re-introducing materialism during the Golden Age, out of nostalgia for the affluent living of previous Ages, was soon to be abandoned.

The attitude to time

Central to the philosophical debates of Tlön was the meaning of Time. Its importance is shown from the great number and variety of philosophical schools that have offered theories about it; from the one that negates time ("the present is undefined, the future has no reality other than as a present hope, the past has no reality other than as a present memory") to the one which believes that "the planet has been created a few minutes ago, furnished with a humanity which remembers an illusory past"[22] or to another that declares that "all time has already transpired and our life is only the crepuscular and no doubt falsified and mutilated memory or reflection of an irrevocable process" or to that which maintains that "while we are asleep here, we are awake somewhere else, and that thus every man is two men", or in fact that every man is many men.

Common to all schools was the aim to relieve life from the burden of time. This ethical aim became one of the main preoccupations of Tlön's education -being considered fundamental to man's happiness and attitude to death. The objective was, ultimately, to disassociate death from time and to abolish fear of death from the hearts of men by insisting on its biological necessity.

Speed was not considered a virtue which is not surprising in a society which was not in the least cost conscious. There was no virtue in completing 'in time' or doing a job today rather than tomorrow or getting to the journey's end fast. The name Ithaca given to the most majestic garden in a city of the southern region is a reference -so writes Ladislas- to the virtue of the enjoyment of the process or the pleasures of the route, a notion later to be found in Homer's Iliad. Speed for the people of Tlön had a *"psychological dimension"*; a better speed was one that would enable a greater pleasure in the undertaking and would eliminate the anxiety about the linearity and irreversibility of time and the sadness about the irrevocability of the past.

To defeat irrevocability of time philosophers used memory as their natural ally. Memory was considered one of the highest virtues, as it was thought to enable reliving experiences which are considered "past". "If there is a method, available to every human being, of witnessing a feeling or an event that had been experienced at some past moment, with all the accuracy of the previous occasion, is that not a proof of man's power over time?" asked one of the fathers of Tlön's idealism[23]. He conceived such seemingly paradoxical notions like "planning or ordering the past" and "remembering the future". It is true that the language of Tlön helped him to formulate these propositions, which to us seem totally absurd (the verbs for *"remembering"* and *"anticipating"* in Tlön's language can be translated as *"looking-in"* and *"looking-out"* respectively). This philosopher performed the "experiment of the black box", now considered a classic, in which he shut himself in a black cubic soundproof room for four days and nights excluding all external stimuli and concentrating his thoughts on a loved companion who had been dead for years. Aurally assisted with taped sounds from the deceased person's life and surrounded by familiar objects affiliated with that person, Hirkkat was trying to prove that, as he was actually re-living a part of his 'past' life during a fraction of time, he had in fact moved back in time during that fraction. He argued, discarding completely physical needs, that, if both his feelings and his imagination were exclusively directed to 'past' experiences, then there was no mental faculty of his that was actually 'living' in the present in the duration of the experiment; so, as the time experienced was not related to the present –and neither could it possibly be future- then it must have been past time.

The corollary of the attitude towards time was that the notions of 'keeping time', of predicting and of making detailed plans about the future were unacceptable. By some they were considered as absurd, by others as unethical[24] and yet by others as causing unhappiness in the sense that worrying too much about the future and planning the next moment takes away the pleasure of living in the present[25]. *'Deferment's praise',* was one of the most eloquent diatribes about the management of personal time; so states Ladislas, but fails to make any reference to its author -whom Amorson believes to be of Ionian descent.

The attitude to death and happiness

The main philosophical school which was concerned with metaphysical questions put forward a hypothesis viewing life and death in terms of a dynamic theory of communication. In the language of Tlön there were no simple nouns for life or death; instead, these notions were conveyed by two verbal constructions, both having the word 'oerm' as their first component (signifying *"moving on a route"*); this common to both notions word was qualified by two attributes: *"in search of wisdom"* for *"being-living"* and *"in search of communication"* for *"being-dead"*.

According to that theory human existence was considered as made up of certain constituent properties that proceeded through time in an increasing or decreasing capacity or quantity. Life and death were seen as the composite processes of gradual quantitative, followed by qualitative, change of these specific properties: for example, the failing of memory, the diminishing clarity and purity of perception and the increasing acquisition of wisdom were seen as, negative and positive respectively, attributes of *"being-living"*. The phenomena of birth and death as instant occurrences in a time-continuum, were, in their language, denoted by the adverbial phrases *"moment-of-moving-from-unknown-to-known"* and *"moment-of-moving-from-known-to-unknown"*, or to be more precise, moment of moving from the field of wisdom-search to the field of communication-search.

As death in its essence is not instant, but progressive, so is a certain speculative insight into the unknown. This insight reaches its climax at the actual point of dying, but there every contact between the two regions (known and unknown) ceases just as the line of the route of life intersects the *"plane of no communication"* (only to re-emerge again at some other moment into the known region).[26]

In the later stages of Tlön's civilisation these metaphysical hypotheses were complemented by their ethical counterparts. The philosophy of death and -according to Theophobus[27], mentioned by Ladislas in his diary- the preoccupation with the subject, even at primary educational level, created optimism rather than pessimism. Familiarisation with death was one of the bases for the acknowledged happiness of the people of Tlön, the elimination of fear and *"the reign of Eros rather than Necessity in the relations among men"*.[28]

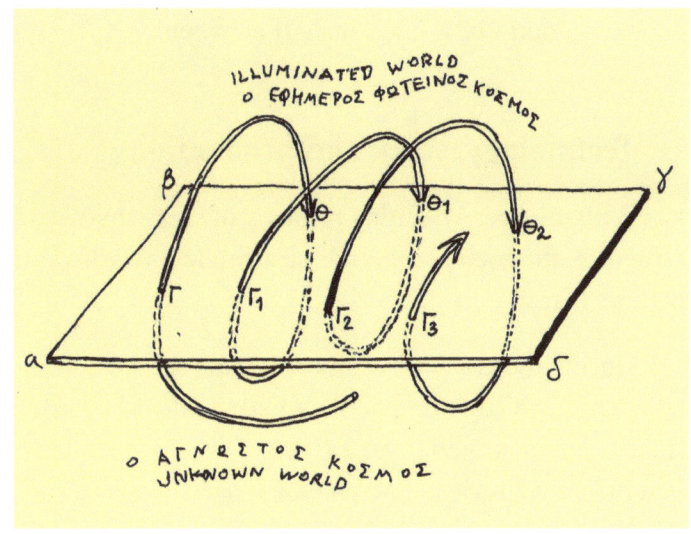

The geometry of Tlön metaphysics

Happiness was so important a subject and so valued an idea that it was not being discussed at all. So was sex. All things or states of mind, that were loved and enjoyed by men, were treated with a mystic reverence. Anyone enjoying these virtuous states should refrain from boasting or exhibiting or impressing his joy onto others. The contrary would be considered not so much a prejudice, but a sign of undignified behaviour towards others and oneself.

Making plans for the future was treated as an ambiguous subject. Some held that, on hedonistic grounds, it had to be condemned, as it takes away the pleasure of enjoying the present by turning our minds to the notion of the arrow of time, to its irrevocability and hence to death; others, from idealistic premises, considered it a blessing, emphasising the important function of expectation and hope on the well-being of men and contrasting it to the *"pedestrian reality"*. *"The wise men (of Tlön)"*, writes Ladislas *"thought of the prospect of happiness as more valid and more pleasurable than happiness itself. They also preached that making plans should allow for vagueness and imprecision. They urged young people to think of the future in hazy images rather than in concrete terms, as they considered that the concretisation of the time element in plans is what renders them instruments of ennui or even desperation".*

One philosophical school taught that happiness is primarily a property of memory (remembering the past) or of contemplation (expecting the future); in other words that when we are enjoying a happy event, we are not really aware of the fact, as enjoyment itself precludes the consciousness of happiness. This comes only at some future time ('how happy we were then'); or the happy state is achieved as precedent contemplation ('how good it shall be when...')[29].

Technology, work and production

With the overwhelming primacy of idealism over all other doctrines it is not surprising that the social structure, the social aims and the attitude towards production and consumption in Tlön were remarkably different from ours.

During the Golden Age the rationale for the continued artificial maintenance of material scarcity and slog work, which had up to then perpetuated the system of domination over people and over nature, was finally demonstrated to be a fraud. This seems to have taken a long time to happen, a time that perhaps had meant centuries of actual wars, uprisings and spiritual battles.

Ladislas, incidentally, describes the ruins of a *"Temple of Victory"* standing in isolation in the middle of a high plateau of roughly circular shape. This was, according to recent archaeological interpretations, "a monument to the defeat of the old technological materialism by the new culture of Eros". Ladislas makes a suggestion, with no great conviction, that the civilization of Tlön followed the historical cycles of Endless Recurrence, as this was the only way to explain certain proofs of unprecedented technical progress. But it was actually Caspar Amorson -viewing things with the advantage of posterior knowledge- who put forward the plausible explanation that, before the Golden Age, Tlön had reached a very advanced level of technological civilisation with remarkable technical achievements and with an enormous capacity for natural exploitation. This, apparently, disintegrated after the massive popular upsurge, instigated by the idealist scholars, priests & philosophers or –which is more convincing- as a result of the environmental breakdown at the end of the second era; this led to the longest and most stable era in Tlön's civilisation, referred to at times as *"the Golden Age"*, at times as *"the Age of Harmony"* or *"the Age of Poets and Philosophers"*. Theophobus, describing the process of change, remarked that *"the new polis had to take a step backwards in order to progress"*[30], a somewhat esoteric statement which perhaps refers to an apparent return from various organizational methods considered as *"advanced"* to others which are thought of as *"primitive"*.

There seems, for instance, to have occurred a "materialistic nausea" at a massive scale, which led to a "voluntary restriction of material needs by all, a return to more communal ways of life and to a modern artisanat, the abolition of wealth and profit as the motivation of productive work and its substitution with justice and the satisfaction of social and psychological needs of men. Every work was art, every production was creation".[31]

To convert Ladislas's literary style to a more factual and explicit one, we assume that the effect of the decentralisation of energy sources enabled all individuals a freedom of control over a true *"people's technology"*, based mainly on natural forces such as wind and sun. The switch from demand for a materially higher standard of living to a desire for a better life had proved the collective uselessness of the previous era, when wasted labour was put into the production of useless products, which were supposed to increase a hypothetical consumers' satisfaction.

As a result, industry -as we know it- was devalued and lost its industrial character. There were large shifts of population and resources from industry to the land. Parallel to the industrialisation and mechanisation of agriculture there was a ruralisation of industry. Technology was so advanced that its importance, its ostentatious character and its publicity rapidly diminished. The same was true about medicine, which reached such an insight into human nature, that most drugs were rendered useless. A few large industrial plants, totally automated, were responsible for the stable production of a limited number of basic *"raw-material"* goods. Most products and particularly those necessary for the sustenance of daily life were home-made, a term which should not be taken to denote primitive technology or means of production. Sophistication of technique was not the prerogative of centralised and specialised industrial process; assisted by the continuous growth of information technology –which made scientific knowledge and its technological applications available to everyone - specialized production was in the hands of everyone and could be achieved in everyone's back garden. So was research, whose methods and means became available to all through the democratisation of information and knowledge. *Do It Yourself* , far from being a crude bedsitter necessity, had been elevated to an art and a way of life.

This was consistent with the prevailing notion that every creation was artistic creation and every creating person –in fact every person- an artist.

Social life as product of non-violence and ideological tolerance

It is perhaps too difficult to imagine today what astounding effects this revolution about the decentralization of energy production must have had on the socio-political structure of Tlön, on its culture and on its spatial expression -and Ladislas is rather obscure on this point except for some sketches that he included in the manuscript's chapter dealing with artefacts. What I can conjecture is that this deep and general change of mentality led to an ideological pluralism, to a power polyarchy and to a genuine elimination of ideological intolerance.[32] Due to material affluence and to its low level in the scale of social values, all *"power struggle"* was limited to the sphere of ideas and since *"ideological struggle"* was thought to be the basic object of philosophy and philosophy was considered to be the main aim in life, intellectual antithesis and conflict were sought after and were elevated to virtues.[33] This again shows the ethical and practical basis of the philosophy of Tlön put forward with disarming simplicity by the pragmatist philosopher Anexikakos: "Peaceful co-existence of races, classes, creeds and conflicting ideologies of all kinds can be achieved, because it is a social necessity and because there is a practical way to achieve it. Every person in Tlön, from almost infancy age, is taught that all dogmas are subordinate to a primal collective principle: adopting tolerance as a life-long discipline in order to avert clashes that can lead to major disasters".

This combination of idealism and of coolheadedness and practicality is very characteristic of the people of Tlön (and, I would think, difficult to achieve to-day). It is significant of the conscious effort to attain balance between idealism and realism that one of the most valued virtues was the ability to keep one's self-awareness alive, to be constantly in a state of mental and intellectual alertness.[34] Apart from self-awareness, attaining a sharp memory and respecting balance were the highest philosophical values and practical objectives. Balance was sought everywhere: between the groups constituting society, in "reconciling intellectual and ethical individualism with ordered social life", between the values of the Greek City state and the need to abide by a new world order, between chance and necessity. Balance was the cardinal value leading to the primordial community goal, Harmony.

Caspar Amorson points out the similarities between Tlön's mainstream practice of general tolerance and various philosophical schools from the Greek antiquity down to seventeenth century English and Dutch liberalism.

This is rather an obvious remark from Caspar. But what is unexpected is his stressing of certain common traits with the teaching of Asoka, the Indian king, who reigned between 273 and 232 B.C. and who, after conquering Kalinga, was so horrified with the aftermath of war, that he embraced Buddhism and dedicated the rest of his life trying to apply Buddhist principles to the administration of his vast empire and to rule according to the Law of Reason[35]. Asoka's *edicts,* mainly concerned with the reforms he instituted and the moral principles he recommended in his attempt to create a just and humane society, were engraved in rocks and stone pillars found scattered in more than thirty places throughout India, Nepal, Pakistan and Afghanistan. Most of them are written in Brahmi script; the language used in the edicts found in the western part of India is closer to Sanskrit although one bilingual edict in Afghanistan is written in Aramaic and Greek.[36] The edicts were discovered in 1837 and identified in 1935.

Transcription of one of the edicts about religious tolerance is characteristic: "Beloved-of-the-Gods, King Piyadasi, (this is Asoka's selected name for himself) honours both ascetics and the householders of all religions, and he honours them with gifts and honours of various kinds. But Beloved-of-the-Gods, King Piyadasi, does not value gifts and honours as much as he values this -- that there should be growth in the essentials of all religions. Growth in essentials can be done in different ways, but all of them have as their root restraint in speech, that is, not praising one's own religion, or condemning the religion of others without good cause. And if there is cause for criticism, it should be done in a mild way. But it is better to honour other religions for this reason. By so doing, one's own religion benefits, and so do other religions, while doing otherwise harms one's own religion and the religions of others. Whoever praises his own religion, due to excessive devotion, and condemns others with the thought "Let me glorify my own religion," only harms his own religion. Therefore contact (between religions) is good. One should listen to and respect the doctrines professed by others. Beloved-of-the-Gods, King Piyadasi, desires that all should be well-learned in the good doctrines of other religions".

Asoka played a crucial role in spreading Buddhism both throughout India and abroad, and in one of his edicts he spoke of its infiltration among the Greeks (Yona), who settled in large numbers in what is now Afghanistan and Pakistan after the conquests of Alexander the Great, although small communities lived there prior to this. Strong cultural relations were established between his kingdom and the neighbouring Greek kingdoms, like Bactria (ruled by Diodotus) and Seleucia (ruled by Antiochos), as is evident from another edict: "Now it is conquest by Dhamma that Beloved-of-the-Gods considers to be the best conquest. And it (conquest by Dhamma) has been won here, on the borders, even six hundred yojanas away, where the Greek king Antiochos rules, beyond there where the four kings named Ptolemy, Antigonos, Magas and Alexander rule, likewise in the south among the Cholas, the Pandyas, and as far as Tamraparni. Here in the king's domain among the Greeks, the Kambojas, the Nabhakas, the Nabhapamkits, the Bhojas, the Pitinikas, the Andhras and the Palidas, everywhere people are following Beloved-of-the-Gods' instructions in Dhamma. Even where Beloved-of-the-Gods' envoys have not been, these people too, having heard of the practice of Dhamma and the ordinances and instructions in Dhamma given by Beloved-of-the-Gods, are following it and will continue to do so. This conquest has been won everywhere, and it gives great joy -- the joy which only conquest by Dhamma can give. But even this joy is of little consequence. Beloved-of-the-Gods considers the great fruit to be experienced in the next world to be more important".

I suppose that Amorson's insistence on this subject is not unrelated to the fact that one of the principal regions explored by Ladislas, which resulted in many discoveries, was that covered by the Greco-Indian Kingdom of Bactria, in what is now Afghanistan and Pakistan, as shown in the chapter about town building.

In Tlön's Golden Age one of the highest philosophical values and ethics was *balance*. This was also applied to "reconciling intellectual and ethical individualism with ordered social life" and, respectively, to attain a compromise between the revered values of the Greek City state with the need and obligation to abide by the new social order. There were findings proving a concurrent peaceful co-existence and prosperity of the two systems, city states on one hand and larger population entities of national character on the other. Of this citizen's double compliance to the law of the city and the law of a world order Amorson points out a precedent from the time of Alexander the Great, reminding us that Stoics and Epicurians[37] were preaching the brotherhood of men[38] and the more radical Cynics declared themselves citizens of the world, not of cities. It was the time that political liberty was bowing to the authority of Alexander's rule over his vast empire. As a reaction, individualism developed and the Stoics taught that a virtuous life could be lived in any state, irrespective of its social circumstances, until a consensus was formed between individualist thinking and social behaviour.

4. THE ARCHITECTURE OF TLÖN

The philosophers of Tlön, as explained earlier, did not conceive of the world as a totality of things existing in space, but as a series of actions in time. Contrary to what might be expected, their architects did not consider it necessary to express change in buildings by actually enabling structural and partition elements to move or by other equally literal ways. For them a space, a building, a place were continually in a state of change by the mere fact that they existed in an ever-changing environment; a building was a totally different entity at sunrise from what it was under the midday sun or under a lead-nebulous sky. A public square with a single cleaner wandering in its vast spaces, barely visible in the rose-coloured dawn light, was a totally different entity from the same square filled with a thronging crowd.

Time-related perception of space

Engraved on a megalithic Urartian 'vishapkar'[39] near Tesebaini, Ladislas discovered some of the principles that apparently pervaded the theories and practice of Architecture in Tlon:

(a). "In spite of the world being successive and temporal (and not spatial) and of knowing that it does not persist in time, we have to think of space as **static** and as **crystallised** in time".

"Literal space mobility and flexibility are the end of space itself", was a well known maxim of

Phramptonius, a revered teacher of architecture[40]. "The more architects are seeing space as ever changing and strive to adapt it to a variety of situations, the more they are unable to form and design space for **any** situation." and "We must be taught how to erect buildings as if they will be forever", were two more quotations attributed to Phramptonius.

Accordingly, it was thought that the drafting, by city planners, of too many alternative scenarios revealed an inability to visualise and to elaborate **any** scenario at all; this practice was considered as proof of low critical faculty that prevents the recognition and selection of the indisputably beautiful synthesis.

Similarly to what happened with nouns in the language of Tlön, the fact that no one believed in the reality of space (as the world for the philosophers of Tlön was temporal) paradoxically gave to its architects innumerable creative possibilities in shaping it. As in literature, where an author could create a poetic object by an infinite combination of adjectives or verbs and monosyllabic prefixes, so it was with architecture. From a common vocabulary of spatial elements constituting the fundamental units/signs of architectural language (a language which was possessed by everybody, not just professionals) combinations were formed in the synthesis of *"spatial objects"* of varying spatial complexity - proportional to the scale of generality of values expressed in the object. Architectural design became a pure play. Among the drawings found in the Manuscript are some sketchy notes of surveys from ruined towns, accompanied by what appear to be "reconstruction plans". Although no comment is offered by Ladislas, Amorson, after spending some time investigating these plans, soon arrived at the conclusion that they are examples of the 'pure play' genre; to which I suppose that anyone with basic knowledge of architectural history shall agree. What I am doubtful about is whether they are genuine Ladislas plans or parodies springing from Amorson's sense of humour.

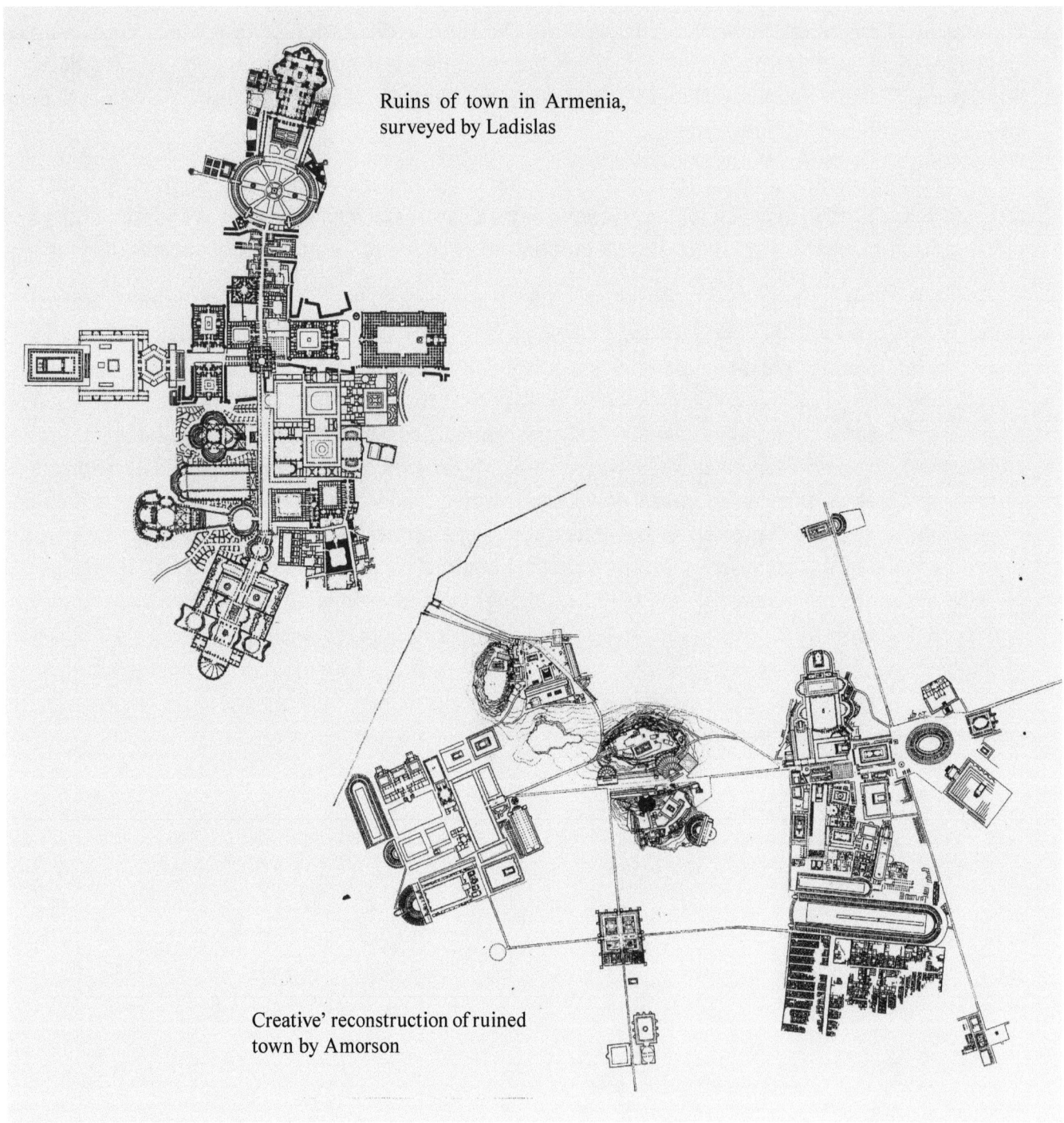

Ruins of town in Armenia,
surveyed by Ladislas

Creative' reconstruction of ruined
town by Amorson

At the beginning of the Golden Age architecture was emphatically treated as a conceptual (often witty) game, an exercise in poetic creation, using the architectural elements in the same way that language was using words. The reason why it became common practice during the early years of the New Age was the reaction to the oppression that architects were subordinated to during the long period of Environmental Authoritarianism. The rules and directives that regulated all the activities of men did not leave architecture -or in fact any human intervention on the environment- unaffected. Extreme examples were rules about the aesthetics of buildings. Ladislas notes the absurdity of an engraving which he discovered: it shows a pillar with two symmetrical fans or wheels; the pillar appears to be quite a sophisticated pylon (resembling a wind turbine), but is decorated in a style reminiscent of a greek doric column. He assumes that this ridiculous form was the result of a "traditionalist administration" imposing ancient morphology aesthetics on advanced technological devices.

(b). "Architects should discard all teleologies"

Working in a social environment frugal in terms of material needs architects were obviously unaware of functional, technological and productive determinisms. Operational needs as we know them today were considered flexible and variable (and man physically a greatly adaptable animal). Operational techniques were never thought of as deterministic of architectural forms: the extremely fast development of technology had surpassed the prestige of technological innovation and the technocratic approach was rendered obsolete by an evolving, advanced, inexpensive and decentralised technology available to everyone.

Buildings would not be considered more wasteful or redundant if they were used and enjoyed by few people -rather than by large crowds- or at few instances -rather than very frequently.

Functionality in the sense that 'form follows function', arising out of material needs, was unthinkable. Instead, architects gave considerable importance to the aspiration-needs and those that are born generally in the realm of spiritual life and psychology.

It is noteworthy that elements of nature (not just trees, shrubs etc., but larger landscapes) were also included in the architectural vocabulary enjoying equal validity with the proper 'spatial', 'structural' or 'tectonic' elements. Natural objects were considered –and used- as spatial elements, totally undifferentiated from 'bricks and mortar'.

Elements of nature were part of the
architectural vocabulary proper

This becomes particularly evident in the architecture of multi-religious temples –which justifies opening a parenthesis on the subject. Ladislas discloses his perplexity from visiting and describing one of these temples:

Open-air multi-creeds temple

"This is an interesting open-air temple which collectively served seven different faiths. Its form derives from two concentric circles. Apparently, the single space within the inner circle functioned both as sanctuary and nave. As there are no signs whatsoever, I am unable to discover the nature of the adoration object, which I suspect was in the centre of the building's inner circle. The outer space between inner and outer circles was the splint, but it reminds me of a purgatory - a preparatory space for introspection before entering the actual temple. This space is sub-divided in seven sectors, one for each creed, arranged in labyrinths by three-yard high masonry walls and served by separate entrances. It feels as if the design implication was that entering the temple is not an easy and simple act, but a contemplative process".

The answer that all seven congregations finally united in worshipping an evergreen tree was given only recently by Amorson using small scale geophysical survey and radiocarbon dating techniques.[41]

The notion of standard needs that would have to be satisfied by standard types of buildings was foreign to the architects of Tlön, as one could not expect to find more than two identical objects anywhere. This was true even in the architecture of dwellings which, as a rule, tended to be modest and common structures. Ladislas describes the admiration of an architect visitor to Tlön[42] about a building in the water edge, whose function was not explicit and which was called what one can translate as House of Contemplation. It displayed an intricate succession of courts, some open, some covered, some totally blind, some with a fenestration designed to enable controlled views to selected natural elements: a large oak tree, a distant mountain peak, an island on the horizon.

Another old teacher of Tlön, Himaerus, left a somewhat cryptographic pronouncement about two distinguished philosophies of architectural form-giving, the Static and the Dynamic; he assigns to them Mass and Space as their basic design substance, and designates Materialisation of Idea and Idealisation of Matter as their respective aim.

(c). "The design of Public Buildings is a collective work; architects act as knowledgeable advisors to the interested community groups".

Architects acted as advisors to the design of public buildings or spaces with the participation of large crowds that met on the spot and would debate for hours the height, plan-angle or texture of a particular wall of the building. Issues such as delay, productivity loss or low profitability of the process made no sense whatsoever. The deliberation about aesthetic matters was most important in Tlön, similar to the contemporary concern about cost of works and materials. The building was an outcome of artistic and spiritual creation and not of labour. The architectural object was always conceived as a work of art. Similarly every action of life was an expression of an aesthetic or a philosophical desire.

Art was not just limited to artists, art collectors and art-addicts. All men created art and consequently the notion of museum or art-gallery in the contemporary sense was irrelevant, as the whole city was a noble museum open to everyone. The population was inspired by the Muses constantly and not just on weekend visits to museums. Every square, every street and every corner of the city was the material evidence and symbol of a historical conflict. Not a belligerent conflict between armies, not a monument to creators of glory and mutilated bodies, but a contest for the dominance of ideas.

The labyrinth

And yet the architectural liberalism evident mostly in the design of residences was forsaken in favour of a canonistic symbolism, when it came to public buildings at the time of the Golden Age, where architecture followed certain rules to be accepted universally with first among them the use of the labyrinthine form. The labyrinth was the generic form for the vast majority of buildings of religious or political function that Ladislas had discovered in his travels.

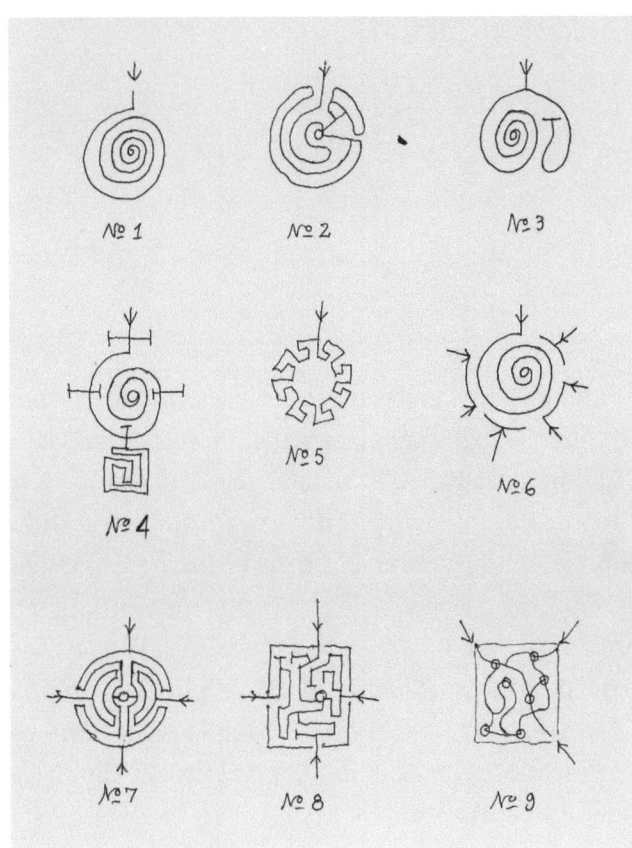

The nine types of Labyrinths

For the builders of Tlön, who exhibited a migthty propensity for architectural allegories, the labyrinth was considered a schema heavy in symbolic content and meaning. Ladislas asserts the existence of a classification of labyrinths –conjecturally attributed by Strabo to Herodotus, after the latter had visited the Egyptian Labyrinth and expressed his admiration of the stupendous edifice.[43]

The classification distinguishes nine types of labyrinths falling under two basic categories, those with one and those with more than one entry points.

The first category includes five types of labyrinths. Type One: Unicursal, a single unbranched access (path) leading to and from the goal (or centre). Type Two: Unicursal to the goal, but more paths from goal presented as alternatives; from these only one leads back to the entry, the rest leading to blind alleys (impasses) or forming loops. Type Three: Two alternative branching paths, one being the real access to and from the goal, the other leading to impasses. Type Four: One access path to goal spotted with nodes from which looping paths or blind alleys branches off. Type Five: There is no goal; one convoluted access path leads back to entry point after branching off to loop.

Under the second category come four types. Type Six: Path from one entry point leads unicursally to the goal; paths from all other entrances lead to blind alleys or back to other entrances. Type Seven: Paths from more than one entry points give access to the goal; paths from other entry points loop unto themselves and return to the entry points. Type Eight: Paths from all entry points give access to goal, but they are spotted with fake forking paths which are either loops or lead to blind alleys. Type Nine: No single goal, but many; paths from all entrances intercommunicate and give access to all goals.

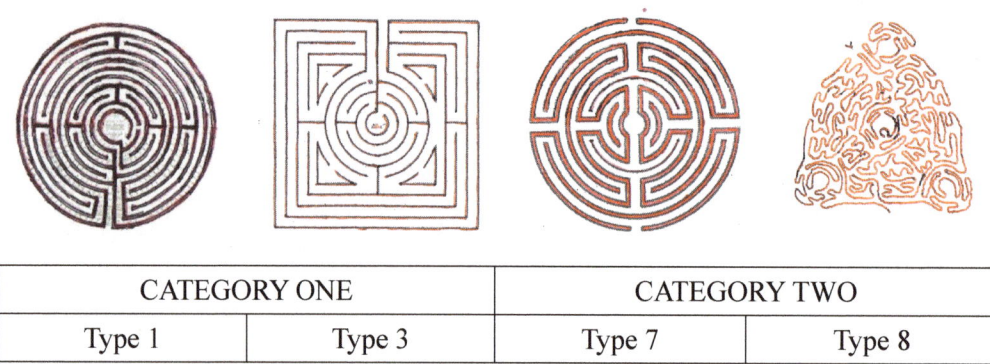

CATEGORY ONE		CATEGORY TWO	
Type 1	Type 3	Type 7	Type 8

Apparently each type of labyrinth described carried a different and specific allegorical meaning pertaining to philosophical issues about fate, free will, chance and time.[44] Their symbolisms and connotations were known to all citizens, so that specific types of labyrinth-buildings had specific meanings, shared by all. For example labyrinth number five could mean: there is no centre and following a path towards a goal is vain, as you may wander and go fortuitously over the same looping path X number of times, before realising that the entry point simply leads finally to the exit. Or take number six, which implies that you may have to try different paths, leading to impasses, before you discover the one and only door that reveals the true access to the centre. Note that if you are lucky to fall upon the true path on your first choice, you will have missed the whole essence of the moral lesson. The allegory of number eight is that no doctrine is recognised as true —over others being false- but that they are all valid as didactic methods of inquiry and investigation; all paths are copious and require toil to perceive their qualities and make your choice.

5. TOWN BUILDING

Caspar Amorson remarks that Ladislas, though keen to describe the philosophy behind the design of towns in Tlön and offering a wealth of information and sources as to its town building history and practice, is rather unclear about the geography of Tlön and about the routes of his expedition and the countries and towns he traversed. His reference to locations throughout the text is perplexing rather than elucidating, so that no-one can actually locate Tlön with indisputable certainty.

The physical environment forming the backcloth of the main fields of his explorations and of the monuments and relics described bears resemblance to two geographical areas. First, the ancient Hourri Kingdom of Urartu, the mountainous area around the lakes Van and Shevan, the sources of Tiger, Araxes, Zab and the basin of river Kura that runs into the Caspian Sea. About the second area Ladislas gives more references in his Diary; from these Caspar Amorson conjectures a route having the Aral Sea as starting point and covering a vast area (extending over five contemporary countries: Turkmenistan, Afghanistan, Tadzhikistan, Uzbekistan, Kyrgyzstan); it includes the Plateau of Ustyurt, continues along the Basin of Amu-Darya (river Oxos in Alexander's time which flows into Aral), then forms a loop along the route marched by Alexander the Great (Bukhara, Karshi, Herat, Kandahar, Ghazni, Kabul, Bactria, Samarkand, Tashkend); the route finally, following the bank of Syr Daria (Iaxartes), ends up again at the Aral Sea.

The broader area of Ladislas expeditions

In some instances references to places spreading over a much broader geographical and historical space (such as Palmyra, Babylon, Luxor, Thebes, Ktesiphon, Taert, Benares, Pataliputra, Topra, Mirath, Laurilla-Nadarigar, Laurilla-Ararage, Knossos, Gournia –and I am omitting a lot) suggest that Ladislas got acquainted with a civilisation of an almost universal outlook, one that covers the totality of the earliest known appearance of city culture, Mesopotamia and Elam, as well as, at least, its first offshoots like Egypt, Crete and the Aegean, Asia Minor and the Hindu River Valley (Harappa). It is evident, that Ladislas had actually visited the aforementioned areas of Urartu and Bactria. It is not clear whether he had direct experience of the Aegean culture, as the Chapter about this region was most probably entirely destroyed by the fire. Nevertheless it becomes clear from the totality of his references, that directly or indirectly, he is dealing with a universal Tlön, both spatial and temporal, covering the antiquity of what some came to term as "the East".

Of particular interest to the geographical framework of Ladislas travels are six maps found in his manuscript, not in the series proper of enumerated pages, but folded and pressed between Books 1 and 2. They are evidently copied from the manuscript CODEX 655, Book VIII, of the Holy Monastery of Vatopaidi on Mount Athos,[45] one of the manuscripts of *Geographia*, the renowned work of Ptolemy, (Claudius Ptolemaeus). A lot of manuscripts of this important work were found in the Vatican and other libraries; it seems that the diffusion of the manuscripts began, according to some scholars,[46] in Constantinople during the last half of the 13th century. This fact suggests that Ladislas may have visited Constantinople in the earlier part of his expedition to the East.

Apart from the copies of the *Geographia* maps Caspar Amorson found, inserted in the manuscript, a printed map illustrating the expeditions of Alexander the Great. The date of the map (1595) suggests that some scholar, most probably a monk, had subsequently been searching to what degree the areas visited by Ladislas coincided with those annexed to the Macedonian empire. Probably this is true for a relatively limited area in and around Bactria and part of nowadays Afghanistan.

In his explorations of the various regions of Tlön Ladislas distinguishes four types of human ecosystems: (a) high plateaus with networks of medium to small helicoidal-shaped towns founded in close proximity to each other, (b) large scale subterranean towns preserved in successive archaeological layers, (c) valley towns along rivers served by major port towns on the river mouths and (d) small hill towns or terraced towns in proximity to seawater or to lakes.

Ladislas distinguishes two plateaus of different size (the first decidedly smaller), dissimilar natural formation (the first more rugged and hilly) and with towns of a totally different concept and form. The one that was probably the scene of his first expedition, which he named, using Greek words, "Υψίπεδον των ‘Ελίκων" (Plateau of the Helices or Spirals) and the other, which he discovered in his second journey, which he called "Υψίπεδον των Χθονίων Ἐρειπίων" (Plateau of Sub-terranean Ruins or simply Ruins). After perusal of the text Amorson concludes, somewhat reluctantly, that the Plateau of the Helices is located somewhere in Urartu[47], whereas the Plateau of the Subterranean Ruins is identified with the high plateau of Ustyurt and the broader area described already.

The Plateau of Helices

The Plateau of Sub-terranean Ruins

Ladislas states that the towns at the Plateau of Sub-terranean Ruins were presumably founded in the Second and Third Historical Ages of Tlön and more specifically during the First Period of the environmental Crisis; they were part of what he terms "armour of technical innovations" (covering their cities with a new layer of 'nature') in which the states invested, at enormous cost, to protect their populations from the environmental and climatic cataclysmic disasters. On the contrary he considered without any doubt that the towns in the Plateau of Helices were creations of the Golden Age. Amorson backs both these theses in a short definitive statement.

The valley towns that Ladislas refers to are most probably located along the river Kura (south of the mountain ranges of Caucasus), which flows into the Caspian Sea, and along the rivers Amu-Darya (Oxos) and Sir-Darya (Iaxartes), both disemboguing at Lake Aral. References to valley towns and port towns as well as to the terraced hill towns of the Aegean are scarce, a fact that may well be due to either the damage of the relevant chapters by fire or to Ladislas's lack of direct experience of these areas and hence to the limitations of secondhand knowledge from other visitors' narratives and from local mythology.

The highest value of towns

Contrary to most civilisations in the ancient East[48], the people of Tlön believed that cities were founded by men, not by gods, and they **knew** that cities developed gradually and were not just created as complete objects in their final form. Nevertheless the prevailing belief was that their structure was based on cosmic symbolism and that gods bequeathed men certain sacred rules, which men should follow in founding cities.

According to this belief the design of human settlements incorporates the primordial god-sent value of balance. Balance is a notion difficult to objectify. In some contexts it stands for harmony; from certain indirect references it was concluded that it also has a connotation of justice, at least in a relative sense: absolute justice is never achieved, but social balance is the aim of justice[49]. So balance is pursued at various levels: balance between design teleology and chance; balance between the various ideological currents of the communities that constitute the society of towns; balance, finally, as a goal of history. The whole history of cities showed a continuous process towards equilibrium. Every remnant of city discovered by Ladislas was a result of a startling interplay between the various concepts of balance and their formal interpretations in space.

The town design principles at the Plateau of Helices….

Ladislas dedicates a large part of his Diary's Chapter 2 to describing the rules applying to the proper design and construction of cities in the Plateau of the Helices, the first type of human ecosystem according to his classification and the only one in Tlön where town building followed an explicit canon. Ladislas maintains that he deciphered the canon from an obscure scripture carved on a stone slab, but reveals no details (Caspar Amorson offered a sketch explaining the geometry of the helix, the basic shape used in tracing the form of towns):

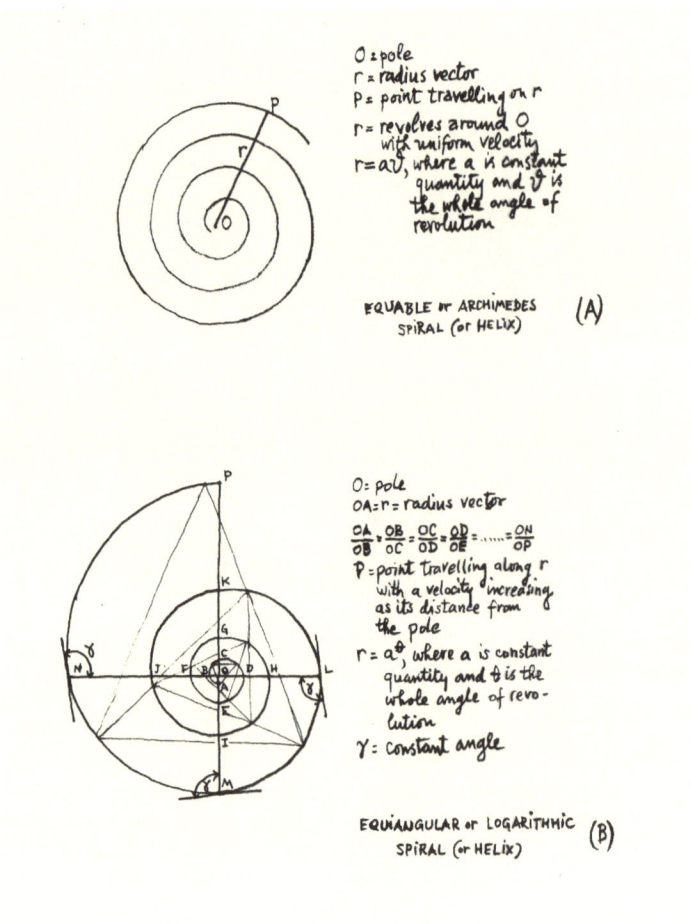

Equable (or Archimedes) helix and equiangular (or logarithmic) helix

- "The form of cities was at first sight apparently chaotic, but at closer and deeper look, the seemingly unstructured city revealed a clear structure common to all cities at the Plateau of the Helices.

- These common elements emanate from an edict setting out clear rules addressed to the founders and designers of towns. The edict was engraved on a renowned plaque discovered in one of the helicoidal cities at the Plateau of the Helices:

- The city is the image in space of an ideal human situation, where groups of individuals live in harmony within a community, this harmony being the **end** of all towns.[50]

- The people of each town will always pursue this end, but no town will ever achieve the end's perfection.

- Whether a town shall finally reach a point nearer or further away from perfection is a matter that depends upon a multitude of circumstances, some causal, some casual.

- As the town's life balances between teleology and chance, its design should, accordingly, allow for these two life-forces.

- In a community exist, now as always, many religions, beliefs, systems and ideologies; these must be able to co-exist and develop; this does not present any risk to the community; on the contrary, it strengthens society.

- The structure of the town must allow the multitude of expressions and endure in time; this means that it must adapt to the unknown circumstances to be created by future generations.

- The structure of the town is the image of its harmonious community, whereas the forms of its parts are the expression of its rich variety of cultures or ideologies.

- It is vain to try to design the form of the town or its details; but it is a necessity to design its basic structure.

- The planning of a town should be minimal. All-encompassing and detailed planning is a frivolous act and hubris to gods.

- The town structure has the geometry of a helix, a shape symbolic of earthly and celestial objects, distinguished for their high formal quality and functional supremacy.

- The helix increases by accumulation, rather than grows; its older parts always remain intact although the total changes, with its history being incorporated in its form.[51]

- The helix is a form identified with life, movement and evolution (ex-helix-is in the Greek language means evolution) and yet we use it to attain its philosophical antithesis, balance.

- A system of straight lines radiating from the pole of the helix[52] subdivide the area of the town in sectors; there are as many sectors as the number of cultural, political or ideological groups that cooperate in the founding of a town, so that each group develops, according to its own code of laws and principles, that sector of the town designated to it."

Ladislas transcribes the written testimony of Cadmion, an ancient geographer and sage describing the founding of a town by six religious sects and philosophical schools who had come to an agreement to urbanise a tract of land on flat ground, somewhere in the Plateau of the Helices.

"The old men, one from each sect, instructed the geometers to define an ecological entity and to survey all important natural elements that constitute it; the streams, the valleys, the gorges, the hills, the rocks, the shrubs and trees, the forested land, the ridges, the slopes.

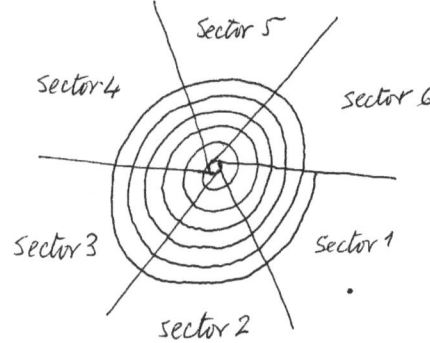

Tracing of a six-religious-sects town

They were then asked to mark out accurately these features on papyrus, which the old men studied as they deliberated about the design of the town. They carefully traced the helix in such a way that they left the important natural features surveyed intact. They then drew radial lines from the pole creating six urbanisation sectors, one for every religious sect. The tracing of the town structure's basic lines on the actual ground was a two-week long intricate procedure of festive and spiritual character. When this was over, urbanisation then began from the pole going outwards, with each founding creed creating its own urban environment within its sector while contributing, at the same time, to the town's Common Centre and to its general spiral-formed infrastructure spine that was concurrently developing."

The refutation of values at the Aegean settlements

At this point in his diary Ladislas opens a parenthesis referring to Chapter 5 of his Diary, where he presents *"the complete refutation of the Plateau of the Helices Town Design Canon"*, propounded by another school of thought apparently rooted in and influential in the Region of the Aegean Islands and Asia Minor. The Chapter was missing from the manuscript pages in my possession and I can only assume that it was lost in its totality, (probably forming a separate volume) in the Covent Garden fire of 1868. Fortunately some fundamental ideas of the Aegean way of town building are revealed by the following fragmented sentences in one of the manuscript's most heavily damaged pages:

"..there seem to exist two types of townships: an earlier one with extremely individualistic character and a later one exhibiting strong community mentality", "[…] seemingly individualistic and anarchic towns, but pleasant and surprisingly interesting", "[…] you conclude that the Aegean towns were permeated by a set of innate unwritten laws, implicit rather than explicit, and lenient rather than dogmatic", "[…] such an approach seems to unleash the creativity of the builder and to give the visitor the joy of surprise.."[53], "[…] many dispersed self-contained tribal(?) or patriarchal family (?) complexes, of mixed productive and residential use, perfectly adjusted to the idiosyncrasies of the ground and charming in their juxtaposed relation to the natural surrounding, which to a large degree is anyway man-made", "[…] they accuse the design of helicoidal towns as mechanistic and teleological –as their evolution is prescribed in their past and their goal is already set at its commencement".

Surprisingly interesting individualistic - anarchic urban sprawl in the Aegean settlements

A rescued and preserved visual impression and quick sketch by Ladislas –copied with an imaginative and restorative intention by Amorson- serves to substitute for some of the missing points of the narrative and to illustrate the artefacts of this Aegean type human ecological environment.

Productive and residential farm settlement
in the Aegean post-industrial era

Extracts from Ladislas's diary (selected by Amorson)

From the profuse remarks, observations and sketches filling Ladislas's diary during his numerous visits to ruined cities, Caspar Amorson proceeded to the following selection, considered as the condensed essence of Ladislas's critical analysis of Tlön's town design and building:

July 1, 1398

"Towns in Tlön were seen as the materialisation in space of a continuous balancing between differing –sometimes even as a compromise between opposed and antagonistic- ideological movements. Towns were the dynamic result of a peaceful social fermentation which always leads to consent and in which all participants are involved by their own free will".

July 2, 1398

"The form of a town mirrors, at each stage of its development, the state of its socio-political dialectics: at some point in time, one ideology thrives and attracts great numbers of people; this has immediate repercussion on urban geography: its urbanisation sector grows faster and extends outwards beyond the limits of others. If this growth persists, and coincides with the ideological -and spatial- stagnation of a neighbouring sector, then the particular sector is allowed –always within limits set by the fear of imbalance- to move and occupy the void of the adjoining empty land -rather than causing an uneconomic one-directional town expansion. This development is known as *metallaxis*".

A town that underwent *metallaxis*

Pre-determined barriers to town growth

July 6, 1398

"If at some stage of a town's development an ideological confrontation could not be resolved by consent and social dialogue or arbitration, then this town fell to disrepute and was gradually abandoned. Hence the considerable number of incomplete cities discovered. Only natural disasters were accepted as legitimate causes of a temporary disorder in the course of a town towards the achievement of balance, in which case the rules of its progress were modified accordingly".

July 7, 1398

"The radial lines separating ideological sectors were both imaginary concepts but also very real. They were boundaries that had to be respected, and could not be built over. They were often used as communal green and shared open space, through which ran the radial roads of the town. The helix on the other hand could not grow indefinitely. In most cases the tracing of the helix led to some physical obstacle, a mountain or a steep hill that was intentionally and from foresight determined, and respected, as a final barrier to the town's growth".

July 12, 1398

"Our guide led us to the ruined city of Karaveh, at the high plateau halfway between Lakes Van and Sevan; this city had been abandoned. From a commemorative plaque embedded on an altar, surrounded by a circular wall, I managed to translate, with the assistance of a local, the ancient engraved inscription: 'The city of Karaveh never achieved its goal; its development escaped the sacred principle of balance. The northern sector founded by the philosophical school of Utilitarians knew a spectacular growth and grew beyond any expectation overpowering its co-founders and spilling over onto adjoining geographical sectors. No town could have of course a felicitous fate, when one social constituent shows such overwhelming dominance over all others. According to our laws the town was abandoned by consent.'

July 18, 1398

"Today I visited Irine in a narrow plain near the valley of Araxes. This was a city that flourished and was successful in reaching a high level of prosperity. Its development was remarkable in the way that it adapted to the changing conditions of its social dynamics. From the street pattern perceived through the ruins I conjecture that there were five founding ideological groups, which up to a time had a balanced development. For lack of information about their teaching I distinguish these groups using colours:

purple, green, mauve, orange. At some point in its history the red and yellow groups ceased to produce knowledge or wisdom, their teaching did not attract new believers and their old believers turned to other philosophical schools. Gradually there was a metallaxis and the degenerating ideologies (red and yellow) gave birth to new ones, the light blue and the dark blue, thus securing the continued development of Irine in conditions of an overall balance".

July 20, 1398

"Deciphering an old text by the radical philosopher Amadeus, I made a most unexpected and, at first sight, disquieting discovery: Amadeus assures that in some eastern region of Tlön, which is not named, towns developed in a spiral form, but their development started from the outer area of the helix and proceeded inward towards the pole! Amadeus explains that in this region's philosophy and mentality geographic centrality was just a geometric characteristic and had no economic 'real estate' connotation. Centrality in town building and the supply of services associated with town centers led to the deprivation of comforts and the curtailing of material pleasures and desires in the first generations following the town's foundation. This abstinence was vested with great moral value. If, after many generations, the urbanisation process ever reached the town's centre (the geometrical pole of the helix), this was acclaimed as a grand social achievement justifying the raison d' être itself of the city's foundation. The apparent irrationality of the process reveals, at a deeper examination, an extremely idealistic conception.[54]

July 30, 1398

"There are two basic types of road in the helix town: the spiral and the radials. Radial roads are called *utilitarian roads*; they take you from point A to point B in a straightforward way, at the same time they keep reminding you constantly of the element of historical time as they lead you by definition from an older to a newer part of the town or vice-versa, depending to whether you drive to or from the centre. The spiral road, on the other hand, referred to as *sectorial* or *recreation or Historical Memory road*, takes you from one sector of the town to the other proving that the town owes its existence only to the effective communication between the different philosophies, cultures or religions that created and developed it.

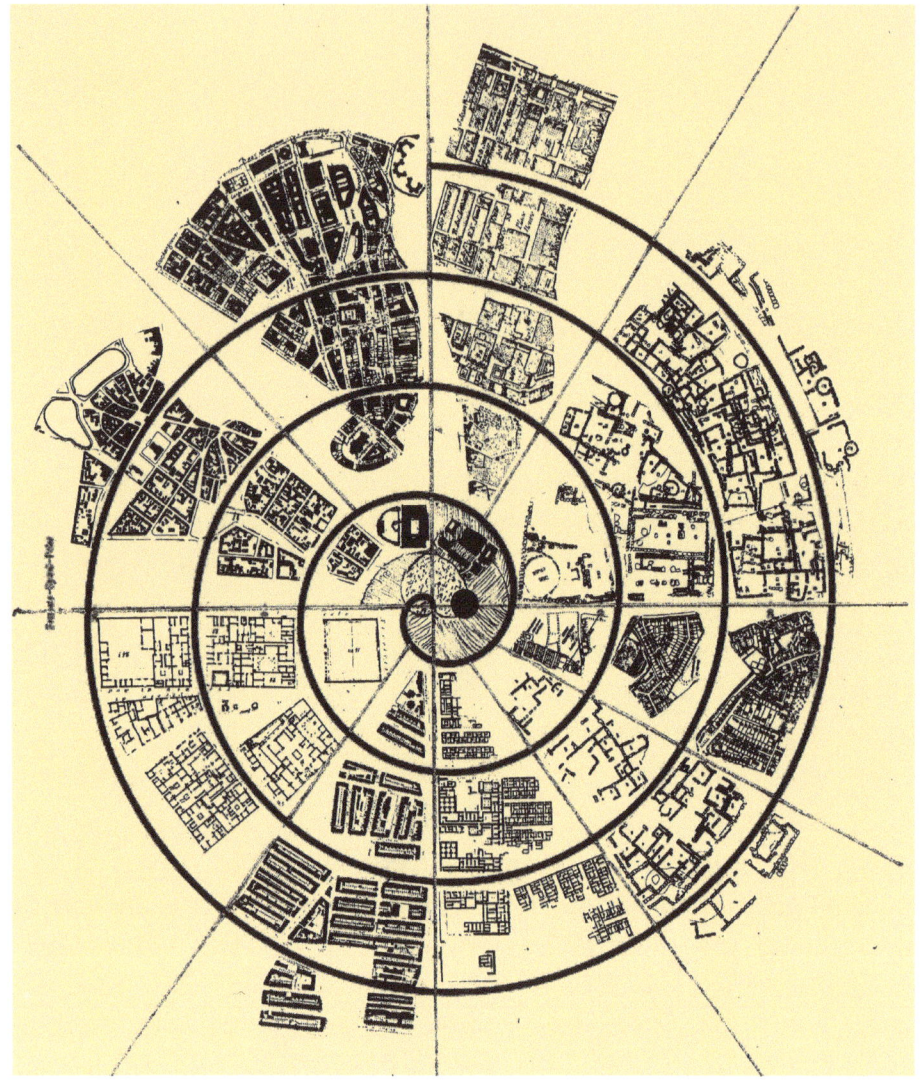

Spiral Town

Sectors of different
urban tissue, history
and character

Independent
growth trends

- but all sectors
harmoniously
subordinated to
common overall spiral
structure and rules

So, whether you walk or ride inwards to the centre or outwards away from it, you do it pondering on and enjoying the collective effort that created the town –and, you are not pressed by time; in fact you have all the time to perceive the essence of the spiritual history of the town. As you visit successive cultural chambers of the town, one after another, you marvel at their corresponding architectural and urban design styles and you appreciate that the diversity of social ideologies results in the formal diversity and beauty of your town".

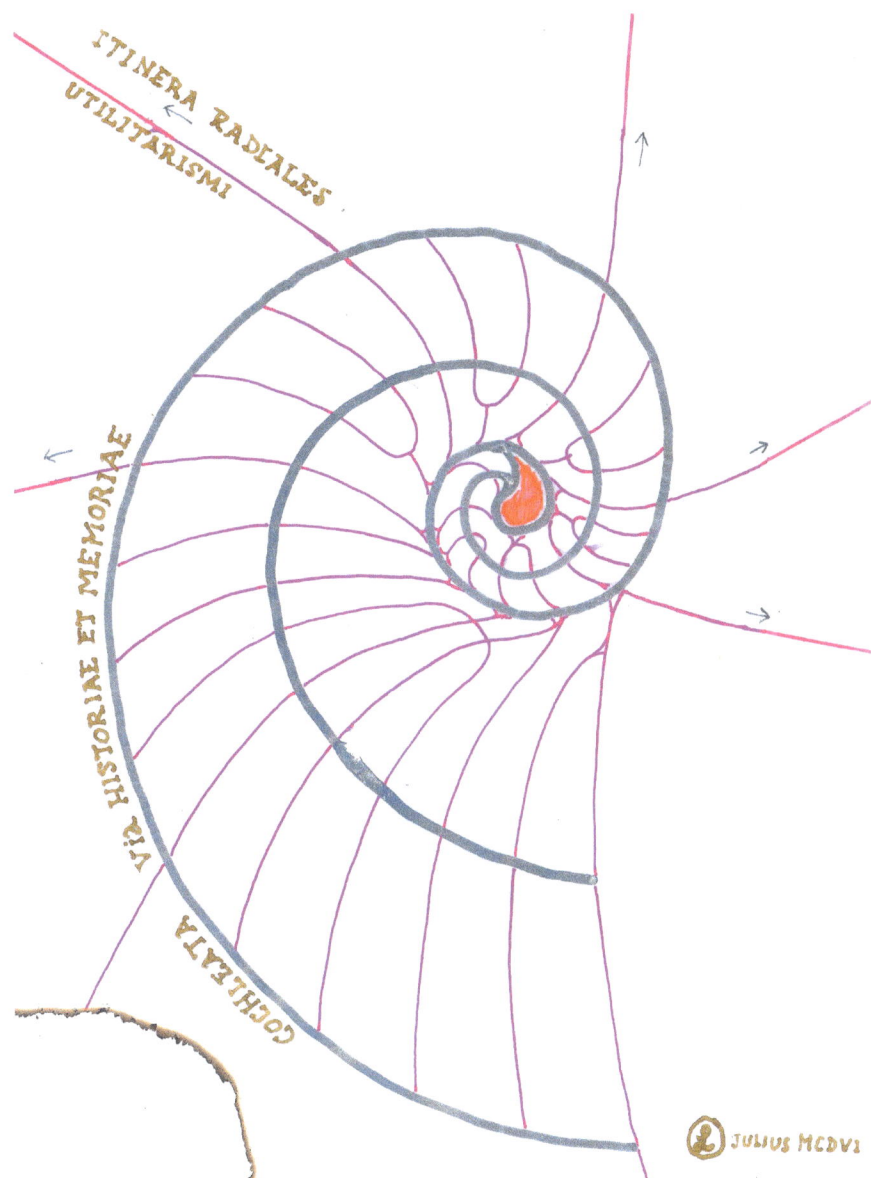

ITINERA RADIALES
UTILITARISMI

VIA HISTORIAE ET MEMORIAE

COCHLEATA

JULIUS MCDVI

Helicoidal town form created by the rotation of two logarithmic helices. Two types of roads are distinguished: in grey, the recreation or historical memory roads; in purple, the utilitarian or radial roads.

August 1, 1398

"Riding my horse on a radial ("utilitarian") road is like going towards the past or towards the future of the town, depending on your direction towards or away from the centre (or vice-versa).

Riding on the spiral ("historical memory") road seems irrational, as it requires from the rider, the coachman or the charioteer a constant course correction in order to keep the carriage on the right track.

Cutting down speed seems a necessity and this is consistent with the notion that speed is defined qualitatively and not quantitatively. I recall with apprehension the inscription on a milestone of a spiral road in one of the cities visited: 'Driving on the road of history requires concentration, masterly skill and discipline', no doubt a literal and metaphorical warning".

September 30, 1398

"I am still in a state of amazement as I write these notes. We have covered in the past two months a vast rugged area lying between the Zagros mountain range in the south and that of Eastern Taurus in the west and innumerable valleys and ravines, with two important rivers and the imposing presence of Mount Ararat felt always above us.

The hill-town of Arshaskun or Tesebaini according to Ladislas

The Arame dam on Zanga river

The locals call this area Uruatri or Uruarti and talk of an ancient civilization. We visited quite a number of ruined towns, all designed on the principles of the helix. One of them impressed me in a most astonishing way. From the primitive diagram encased in the wall of a sacred ruin I infer that the town is Tesebaini.[55] It is built on a low hill, almost a mound, sitting in the middle of a valley, located to the south west of a mountainous landscape with successive ridges and peaks vanishing in the horizon. It is remarkable that the mountain slopes, even steep ones, are meticulously terraced, cultivated and irrigated by an amazingly intricate and ingenious system of canals.

The hill-town with the Arame dam

Pencil drawing by Ladislas

Water is collected at a dam, built at high altitude about 1/3 of a league away, and, channeled through an underground canal, reaches the top of the hill-town and rolls down an artificial spiral river bed. This Water Way substitutes the typical helicoidal road ('Historical Memory Road') witnessed in other helix-towns and allows movement by barges and shallow boats, but only in an outward (and downward) centrifugal direction. Moving to and from the central hill, whose circular ruins indicate the existence of a walled acropolis, was secured via the radial roads, which crossed the Water Way with numerous arched bridges. Irrigation canals carry it to the terraced orchards and vineyards on the mountain slopes".

October 22, 1938

"In two of Tlön's cities I witnessed a series of huge masonry structures, in the form of a T, erected along the axis of the spiral road; could they be relics of an arched way for processional festivities celebrating a deity? Were they perhaps busts of eminent persons fixed at the centre of the structures' tops with the wings symbolising open hands? But no, these busts would be too high to allow good viewing by passers-by. Were they probably supports used to hang awnings covering the stalls of an open market? But this function contradicts the use of the spiral as a thoroughfare. No doubt these structures are a trace of an important function, but no source available offers an explanation that deciphers their use".[56]

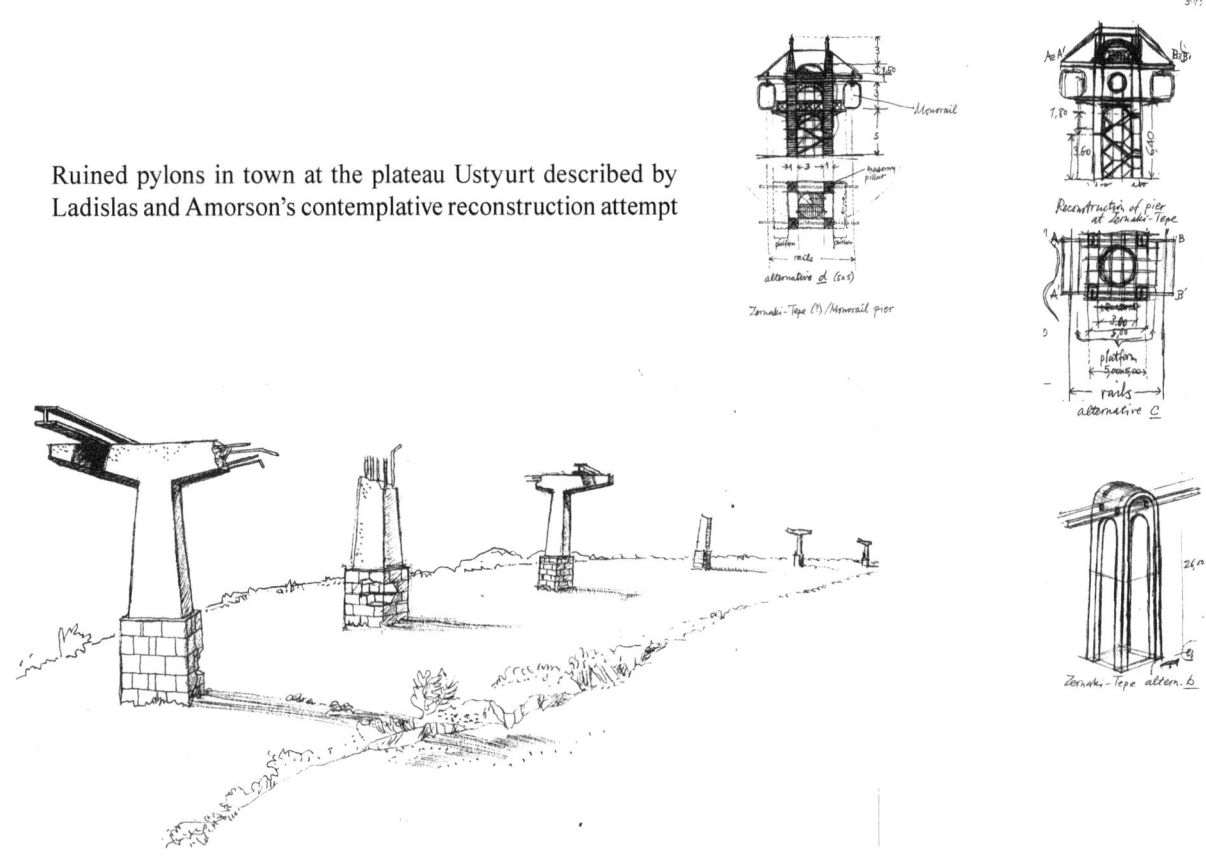

Ruined pylons in town at the plateau Ustyurt described by Ladislas and Amorson's contemplative reconstruction attempt

October 28, 1398

"My narration of the Helicoidal towns visited would be incomplete had I omitted to refer to an engraved geometric design showing the transition from helix to labyrinth; a copy of this I present" .

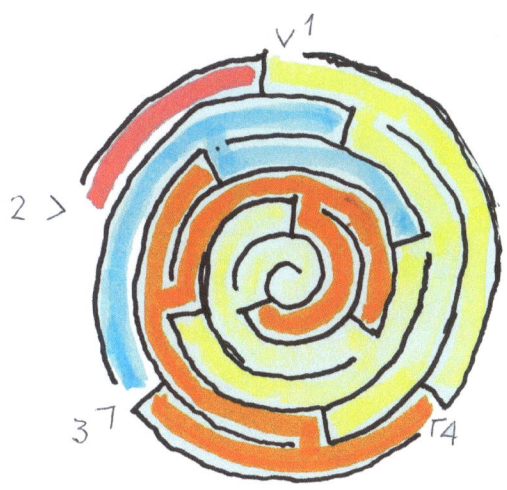

Transition from Helix to Labyrinth

The towns at the Plateau of the Subterranean Ruins

August 3, 1403

"This was the day of my first exploration of a plateau at the central region of Tlön, somewhere in Karabil.

We set off from a village near Samarkand on an expedition which, according to Mazur, our guide, would take up to twenty days. We started our journey in good weather and under clear sky, but… the prospects when reaching the altitude of the plateau were for hot days and very cold nights.

Our group consisted of Mazur, two sentries from the tribe of Turambad and myself, and two horses carrying all our provisions and our shelter kits.

My first view of the Plateau was from a barren and rocky mountain pass; it was breathtaking.

View of the ruins at the Plateau of Helices

Feelings of wonder and amazement overtook me. Enormous ruined metallic structures, forming pure geometrical solids, gaped at the sky in their eternal loneliness. They stood dispersed at almost regular distances of about five to seven stadia from each other, over the large expanse of long-deserted farmland and smoothly curved hilly landscape that disappeared in the horizon. The whole spectacle emitted a sense of weird, almost morbid calmness.

Vast subterranean urban spaces under the artificial nature

Amazement turned into total astonishment when my subsequent archaeological digging expeditions revealed that, to a very large extent, this beautiful landscape was but an artificial, seemingly natural, ground, constructed over the original layers of nature and of human installations and settlements lying beneath. A vast area of urban space, totally covered by this 'artificial nature' (miraculously real and indistinguishable from 'natural' nature) extends underground. The people of this unknown civilization created spaces, where it is difficult to distinguish one element (the tectonic) from the other (nature), as they are both intricately entangled with each other forming a prototype synthesis. I witnessed a few such spaces of indeterminate function around the entry to the subterranean city.

To explore the city's artefacts, its infrastructure and its limits, goes far beyond my, and any contemporary expedition's, capacities. It is simply unthinkable that a civilization as old as the evidence shows could command such overwhelming power, both material and organizational. I am even reluctant to recount this experience lest I am taken as a jester. Decidedly I must strive to organize another expedition next year, this time accompanied by a selected group of wise men, a numerous army of labourers, and ample material and financial means, which will allow me to undertake extensive digging.

Nevertheless a multitude of question marks fills my mind and awaits for answers: How did this fact remain in obscurity for so long and how did it not become more widely known? Did the people of Tlön cover a whole Age of their historical past to safeguard it from the ravages of time? Did they consider their ancient artefacts so valuable? What were the causes that forced them to execute such a costly enterprise that reaches the limits of the superhuman? Did the sun perhaps (or the rain) turn from blessing to immense calamity, one that threatened their civilization and their cities?[57] Did they rely on slave labour or were the resources of their technical civilization so advanced as to surpass even our contemporary imagination?

I named this plateau, I think appropriately, Plateau of the Underground Ruins, using deliberately the Hellenic form Χθόνια Ερείπια, as the word Χθόνιον insinuates demonic powers, and I can see nothing positive in a subterranean city, but only a creation of destitution and crisis[58]".

Amorson treats the subject of the Subterranean Ruins, as the reader can guess, with utmost seriousness, formulating the hypothesis that human societies had to protect their ecological environments from the calamities of a deranged climate and the enmity of nature during the Ecological Crisis Era. Amorson clearly dates the city planning of the Plateau of the Subterranean Ruins at the Second Period of the Era, when the Environmental Wars were already in action, whereas he considers the cities and the city culture developed in the Plateau of the Helices as dating from Tlön's Golden Age. He also supports the view that in some regions of extremely advanced technology —where decentralization of energy production did not take place- human communities had attempted massive organized abandonment of the planet for space destinations. This he based on the frequent finding in subterranean edifices of engravings of a schematic bird-like form reminiscent of spacecrafts.

The Agora

In September of same year 1403 Ladislas visits yet another location at the Plateau of the Subterranean Ruins, a site of extended and elaborate ruins, which he insistently identifies with the enigmatic city of Zernaki Tepe. Assuming he was right (there are some doubts whether Ladislas interpreted correctly his geographical facts) this contention constitutes a serious refutation of the orthodox archaeological thesis that "the construction of the town was never completed."[59] From the description that follows, one presumes that —if the ruin described is Zernaki Tepe- not only was Zernaki Tepe completed, but it had also been the seat of a power, whose remnants suggest a high-level civilisation and prosperity. Strangely, although in the Plateau of Subterranean Ruins, the Agora was built on the original ground level, not covered by the 'artificial nature'.

"We arrived at noon; it is the 5th of September in the year 1403.

I walk in the heart of the city among the ruins of what appears to be its agora, although this differs from every agora to my knowledge, whether classical Greek, Hellenistic or Roman.

The landscape is tranquil; two moderate mounds slightly rising –about ten to fifteen yards- above the general flat ground level, are located, one to the north the other to the south, at a distance of about three and a half stadia[60] from each other. A rivulet with varied plantation on its embankments crosses the grounds mid-way between the two mounds.

A broad paved avenue, about 20 -23 yards wide, joins the two mounds, forming the N-S axis of the agora. Bridging over the rivulet, at its lowest level, the avenue gradually ascends to the level of the mounds with sets of easy steps, symmetrically situated along its course. Three secondary avenues cross the main one on an E-W direction. On both mounds stand two large edifices: the one at the north end of the axis is just a pile of rubble; one can discern only the remnants of the podium. Both have an identical square plan measuring approximately 114X114 yards.

At first sight the formation of the agora is incomprehensible: the relatively small structures (some of them open-air labyrinths of moderate size) located at the ends of the avenues or standing at significant points along them, are completely out of proportion to the immense public open space, which was obviously designed to contain massive crowds that probably participated in political meetings or religious ceremonies. But what were the destinations of all these people, was it only the two imposing edifices at the main avenue's ends? Were there no more covered or interior spaces to receive these crowds?

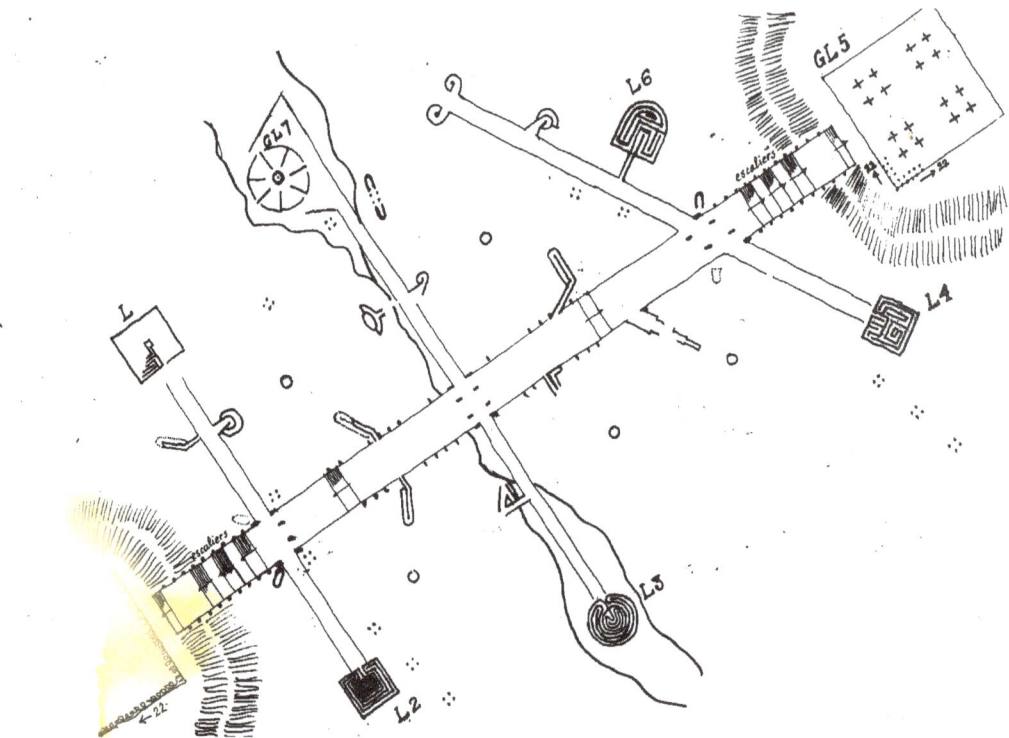

Ladislas' survey drawing of the Agora

Another element that further aggravates the intelligibility of the agora's structure is the series of enormous ruined portals consisting of four square masonry pillars crowned at their top (~12 yards high) with a dome and supporting a platform at an intermediate level, about 5.5 yards from the ground. The portals are reminiscent of the mega-structures that I discovered among the ruins of other cities.[61] One naturally suspects that there were more such portals from the ones found standing today, but they were erected at odd places and their location seems haphazard and not obeying any visible rule. Trying out with tracing lines and joining the portals' positions in space resulted in totally meaningless and erratic courses, not leading to any realistic hypothesis about their scope and function.

A more attentive examination reveals the answer and puts the form of the agora back into rational perspective. Each of these moderate, or in cases minimal, structures functions as portal or trapdoor or light well or shaft or funnel, expressed in imaginative and sculptural form, that enables vertical communication with a vast underground space of a surprisingly elaborate and complex architecture; all underground spaces use the labyrinth as the generic form in the design of their entrance or beyond that. (I asked Aristippos, the Greek orthodox monk who accompanies me, to draw sketches of the space. I am afraid that his work was mediocre and not accurate; so I had to redraw the plan taking into account the topography and scale of the area. Even that did not produce anything more demanding than a rough sketch which explains the concept of the whole idea and presupposes a lot of hypotheses).

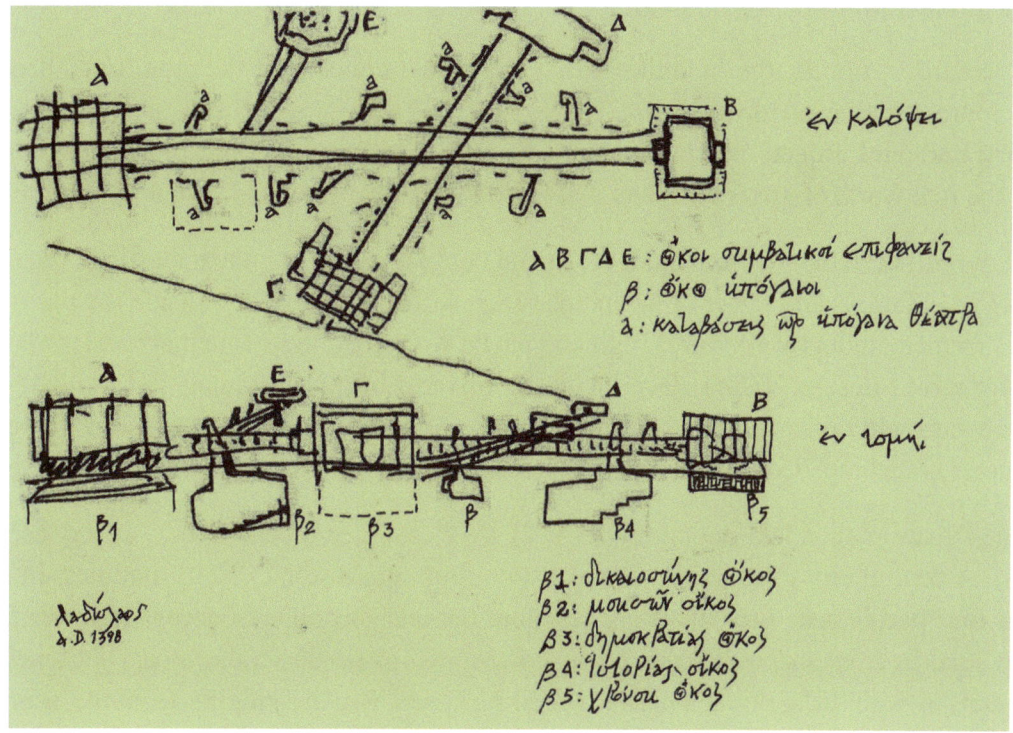

Sketch of the Agora by Ladislas

This then is a public space playing with the notions of visible vs.invisible or apparent versus substantial. What is visible on the surface is only a symbolic super- structure, a sign and an entry point to the reality and importance of public life that takes place at the extensive spatial infra-structure, which is provided, for some unknown reason, at underground level.

Judging from inscriptions carved on the portal structures, I realise that this gathering of installations is the spatial manifestation of all institutions considered valuable and important by the society that flourished on this land at an undefined historical past. Among the inscriptions carved on slabs, whose broken pieces I managed to put together, I read: Οίκος της Δημοκρατίας, Οίκος Δικαιοσύνης, Χρόνου Οίκος, Μουσών Οίκος, Οίκος της Ιστορίας[62]. There are seven more signs unintelligible or destroyed. Descent in three of the infra-structures, in which I was able to enter, left me with the same impression, that there is a unique relation between the feelings aroused by the perception of the super-structure and that imparted by the corresponding underground spaces –which in all cases are, partly or totally, designed on the labyrinthine form.

I shall venture to proffer the hypothesis that the whole concept of the Agora at Zernaki Tepe is a symbolic representation of Idealism in Civic Space. The visible structures at the surface represent the transitory **material objects** perceived by the **Senses**; but these are only images of –and doors for accessing - the real world of **abstract ideas** that lie in a subterranean level, where **Reason** prevails.

I visited the edifice at the southern mound, which I could imagine as quite majestic .It is a περίπτερον[63] with some of its columns, and fewer of its entablatures, still standing intact. Inside the perimetric stoa a vast space is formed, about twelve yards high and paved with grey and white marble slabs laid out on an intricate labyrinthine design. Visitors faced with the vastness of this absolutely flat 'salle de pas perdus' must have felt –as I felt- rather discouraged from entering and wandering in it, as if some force froze them at the perimeter and compelled them to stand still and perceive the immense space with awe.

The large square plan is laid out on a grid of 21 by 21 squares/modules (measuring, each about 5.4 X 5.4 yards). A central cross subdivides the plan into four squares of 15 X 15 modules, in each one of which stand four portal structures, marking an equal number of points of access to lower floors. From one of these, that had the shape of a nun's hat, I attempted to go down the broad but tenebrous spiral staircase. I arrived with difficulty at a dark low-ceiling space, which –judging from the number of steps that I descended- must be more than eight yards below the ground floor level.

When my eyes got used to the twilight I realised that I was in a labyrinth of ceiling-high walls that created an eerie atmosphere. After some wandering I came to a long corridor running along the perimeter of the square, barely lit from indirect sources, and lined up with a series of square rooms, about 5.4 X 5.4 yards. I entered one room; the side to the corridor had no wall, whereas the other three walls were totally covered, from floor to ceiling, with a square micro-grid (made from a hard unidentifiable material) forming innumerable niches; in these, identical in size and shape semi-precious stones were embedded. Some of these jewels were found missing, no doubt extracted by travellers, who cherish the collection of mementos from antiquities.

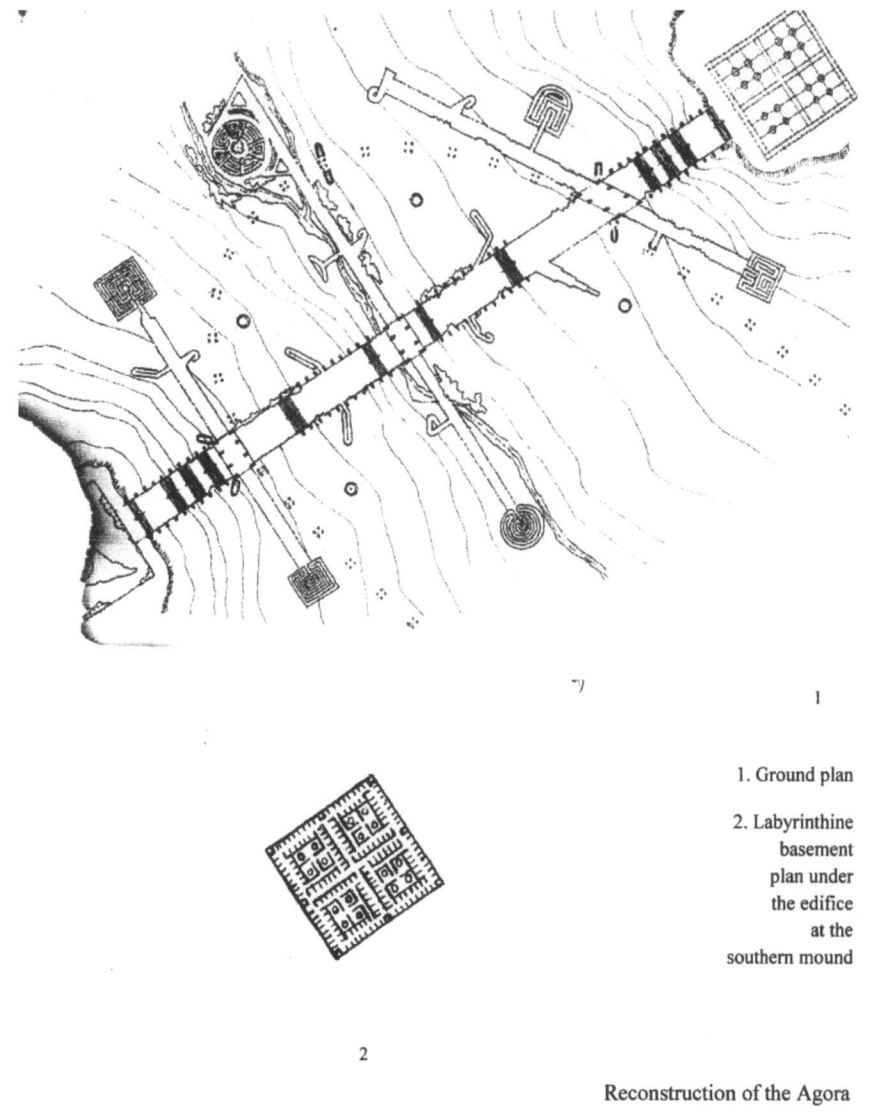

1. Ground plan

2. Labyrinthine basement plan under the edifice at the southern mound

Reconstruction of the Agora

I entered a second room along the corridor and found it had an identical arrangement, and then a third and a fourth. To my surprise all rooms were replicas of a typical room: all three walls of all rooms (on this floor there are 180 such rooms) were lined with the mysterious micro-grids filled with the equally mysterious inlaid jewels. I calculated that each room contained 60000 jewels, bringing the total for the spaces on this floor to 10.8 million.

My final discovery was that there were vertical shafts from this basement level as well –but they are totally and perfectly sealed- and this raises questions as to how many more subterranean levels are probably lying below and to what possible use.

The use and meaning of this building eludes my rationale and my imagination. Its qualities are exceptional: austere geometry, repetitive space arrangement, symmetry, lack of any decoration whatsoever, darkness or very weak indirect light (as if there were no need for natural light). I would have thought the edifice served a very practical purpose, if it were not for its careful and exact –and somewhat contrived- geometry, so I ventured certain explanations about its function: a sanctuary to some God of computation; an enormous receptacle for valuables, perhaps a kingdom's treasure assuming that the stones had numismatic value (but then anyone could conceive other more expedient spatial disposition for such a repository); an expensive artefact for the enactment of massive religious initiation rites; a prison of sinister effectiveness and cruelty; a store for the safeguard of some indeterminate valuables imprisoned, for unknown reasons, in subterranean chambers for eternity. True, though the scope differs, there is an analogy in aim between inanimate objects preserved in a vault and animate beings displaced in a prison: they are both to be kept out of reach, protecting the objects from those outside in the former case and protecting those outside from the inmates in the latter. This is a dominant hypothesis: I believe that this labyrinth was conceived and designed as a place of imprisonment. The question remains who or what was being imprisoned and why."

This was the last entry in Ladislas's diary.

Asked by me to attempt a revision of the reconstruction of the Agora drawn by Ladislas, Caspar Amorson was more than willing; he produced an amended plan which integrates, in an intelligible way, all the fragmented written and drawn information given by Ladislas.

But Caspar's main interest lies in the windowless rooms in the basement labyrinth with their walls lined with precious stones; this intrigued him and he dealt with this matter with researcher's fervour. Amorson believes that Ladislas came face to face with a specially designed storage space for codified data, that the precious stones are some form of computer chips. The civilization of Tlön, facing an Armaggedon and the end of time, took measures to record the totality of its history and culture and to safeguard it for survivors. Ex-Secretary General of UNESCO Kim Il Koon was so taken by this hypothesis --put forward to him by Amorson during the Geneva Conference on the World's Culture, 1984-- that he financed the first expedition in the mountains of Armenia, headed by Amorson himself, to produce some evidence. Other Archaeological Schools followed and are still busy to locate and reveal this cultural depository. I know from first hand that Amorson was working hard to organize a second expedition, this time in Afghanistan, but the war interrupted his plans putting them in abeyance for an indefinite period of time.

One final but crucial question hovers: if Tlön reached its Golden Age, why is it extinct?

This is, literally, another story.

NOTES

1 Jorge Luis Borges: "Fictions" – J. Calder, London 1965.

2 Borges, p. 30.

3 Borges, p. 32.

4 Borges, p. 21.

5 At the time Lithuania was an important player in the European map, extending gradually from the North Sea to the Caspian (in the years 13oo, 1316-41, 1345-77 and after its union with Poland in 1386). Lithuania was converted to Christianity in 1387.

6 According to Andre Maurois, in his Preface to *"Labyrinths"* by Jorge Luis Borges, New Directions, N.Y., 1964

7 The diary is, somewhat inappropriately, headed "TALES OF LITHUANIA".

8 Had Ladislas been living in our age, he would have no difficulty in recognizing the two terms: 'ecological' and 'sustainability'.

9 With this periphrasis I translate the term «τεχνολογία» used by the unknown author.

10 Ladislas quotes Promachus, a philosopher of the Aegean culture. Amorson points out the rather obvious fact that Promachus was describing the symptoms of global warming and the greenhouse effect and their consequences on nature and on life on the planet

11 The Gospel according to Matthew, chapter 5, verse 39: "But as I say to you do not resist one who is evil. But if anyone strikes you on the right cheek, turn to him the other also".

12   Amorson prefers Environment Wars to Land Wars.

13   Nigel Ferguson, *'The Nation that fell to Earth'*, TIME magazine, Sept. 11, 2006.

14   A term used by Franz Fanon.

15   P.C.Liarson in his PhD thesis 'Olethros- the Neomartyrs of Christianity' (University of Lund, 1991) refers to the existence of Christian fundamentalist groups, among which most active was a body of self-sacrificing kamikazis, founded by the fanatic prophet Jesus-Maria Peisithanatos, on the same lines and rationale as those of Islamic martyrs.

16   Manichaeism: the belief that the world is ruled by two opposing forces, light and dark or good and evil, founded by the Persian heresiarch Manis or Manes in the 3rd century A.D.

17   The Summa Project could not have been effected without the Survey and Monitoring Instrument designed to record and assess the physical, mental and psychological capacities of individuals. These data were continuously brought up to date by a massive and extravagant system; thanks to that the *"planning stations"* in each community, parts of the universal planning network, were constantly cognizant of each individual's evolution in anyone's basic conditions, capacities or behavioral patterns and were able to alter the individual's productive role and consumption profile so that the targets of the Collective Plan remain immanently unimpaired.

18   C. Amorson quoting historian and pragmatist philosopher Anexikakos, probably of Hellenic descent or education.

19   Borges, p.22.

20   Borges, p.23.

21   Borges, p.24.

22   Borges, p.25 and B. Russell, *The analysis of mind*, 1921, p.159, quoted by Borges, p.25.

23   Amorson identifies him with the somewhat legendary figure of Hirkkat. See Caspar Amorson, *A first reading of 'the Ladislas Manuscript'*, Annual Review of Scandinavian Studies, Copenhagen, 1998.

24   A notion which is not unlike the 'hubris' of the ancient Greeks; 'might they', wonders Cornelius

Halstroem , Professor of Philosophy in the University of Lund and a friend of Caspar Amorson , 'have been influenced by the philosophers of Tlön?'

25   The idea is described by Bertrand Russell in *"In Praise of Idleness"*.

26   It is interesting to note that *"falling asleep"* in the language of Tlön was conveyed by the construction *"recurrent-moving-from-known-to-unknown"* and *"waking up"* as *"recurrent-moving-from-unknown-to-known"*.

27   Theophobus is referred to as a philosopher and historian in a text attributed to Archias in the Antiochia Archives (Antiochia ad Orontem).

28   A theme found in many thinkers from Plato to Marcuse.

29   This particular belief of happiness has affinities with certain renown philosophical views, as the following survey shows: Aristotle: "Happiness lies in virtuous activity, and perfect happiness lies in the best activity, which is contemplative" Plato: "The greatest happiness (and likewise the greatest virtue) is available only to the philosopher" Plotinus: "Happiness is derived from thought and imagination" Epicurus: "The most pleasant life is one of abstention from unnecessary desires, being content with simple things and achievement of inner tranquility (**ataraxia**) through philosophical conversation and contemplation" Epictetus & the Stoic ethic: "I cannot make A virtuous, because his virtue depends only upon himself; but I can do something towards making him happy, or learned, or healthy" Bentham & the Utilitarians: "When two men's interests clash, the right course is that which produces the greatest total of happiness, regardless of which of the two enjoys it or how it is shared among them" J.L.Borges: "I have sometimes suspected that the only thing that holds no mystery is happiness, because it is its own justification"

30   Caspar Amorson, *A first reading of 'the Ladislas Manuscript'*, Annual Review of Scandinavian Studies, Copenhagen, 1998, p. 83.

31   Theophobus, quoted by Ladislas.

32   According to Russell the most serious cause of wars and violence.

33   Alfred North Whitehead marked in *'Science and the Modern World'* that the confrontation between dogmas is not a calamity, but an opportunity.

34   This is again a notion that reappears also in Greek philosophy and literature, particularly in Homer, who says that the greatest sin was ATH, the loss of that alertness.

35   Caspar Amorson, p.24-27.

36   *The Edicts of King Ashoka – an English Rendering* by Ven. S. Dhammika, BUDDHIST PUBLICATION SOCIETY, 1993, Kandy Sri Lanka

37   Epicurus in 'Διογένης Οινοανδέας,' απ. 30 : 'Καθ' εκάστην μεν γαρ αποτομήν της γης, άλλων άλλη πατρίς εστίν, κατά δε την όλην περιοχήν τούδε του κόσμου μία πάντων πατρίς εστιν η πάσα γη και εις ο κόσμος οίκος' (And of course due to the way the earth has been subdivided one has his country and the other has another; but our world is circumscribed within a perimeter, so that we all have one country, the whole earth, and thus the world is our common home). Επίκουρος, Εκδ. ΘΥΡΑΘΕΝ, Athens 2000, page 232.

38   Socrates is also said to have declared, "I am not only a citizen of Athens, I am also a citizen of the World".

39   A type of menhir (standing monolith) found in mountainous areas of Armenia, dating from pre-18th century B.C.

40   Caspar Amorson, *Addendum to 'the Ladislas Manuscript'*, (Chapter *'Notes on the Architecture of Tlön'*) Annual Review of Scandinavian Studies, Copenhagen, 2001.

41   Another case where a tree (the Tree of Life) occupies the place of divinity is the Vaikuntha-mandala, the celestial abode of Vishnu, depicted as a square patio within a square building with twelve gates facing the four cardinal points (an arrangement of remarkable similarity to an 11th cent. miniature of Jerusalem) (from Titus Burckhardt *'The Heavenly Jerusalem and the Paradise of Vaikuntha', in:* Studies in Comparative Religion, Vol. 4, No. 1 (Winter, 1970). © World Wisdom, Inc. www.studiesincomparativereligion.com)

42   Amorson's research discovered a similar picture in a manuscript by 10th century artist Navarro de Guipuzcoa, but could not trace a connection between the two.

43   Although nowhere in the works of Strabo or Herodotus did I come across any such reference.

44   "In all these stories we find roads that fork, corridors that lead nowhere, except to other corridors, and so on as far as the eye can see. For Borges this is an image of human thought, which essentially makes

its way through concatenations of causes and effects without ever exhausting infinity, and marvels over what is perhaps only inhuman chance. And why wander in these labyrinths? Once more, for aesthetic reasons; because this present infinity, these 'vertiginous symmetries' have their tragic beauty. The form is more important than the content." Preface by Andre Maurois, in Labyrinths Selected Stories and Other Writings, by Jorge Luis Borges, A New Dimensions Book, N.Y. 1964.

45   CODEX 655 is one of the manuscripts of *Geographia* -renowned work of Ptolemy, (Claudius Ptolemaeus), an astronomer, mathematician and geographer from Alexandria (2nd century A.D.), who created an ambitious panorama of oecumene. Of this work various manuscripts were produced, such the Vaticanus Graecus 191, the Fragmentum Fabricianus Graecus 23, the Urbinas Graecus 82, the Seragliensis 57, the Fabricianus Graecus 23.

46   Leonora Navari, *Claudius Ptolemaeus, his Geographike Hyphegesis, and the Ptolemaic problem*, in "Claudius Ptolemaeus Geographia, CODEX 655 of the Holy Great Monastery of Vatopaidi on Mount Athos, Introductory Texts", publ. MILITOS, Athens

47   Probably in an area around lake Sevan, between the rivers Araxes and Kura. The area is too rough and mountainous to qualify as a plateau, unless Ladislas describes a land confined within very narrow limits. I have my doubts about the location and I am more inclined to believe that the Plateau of the Helices lies north of the river Kura.

48   The city for most early civilisations was in the image of God. Four sources are given, one from Egyptian mythology (a), one from Sumeria (b), one from Babylon (c), and one from Genesis (d):

(a)   Theology of Memphis, Egypt (7th cent. B.C., based on a text more than 2000 years older): *"... and so Ptah was satisfied, after he had made everything as well as all the divine order. He had formed the gods, he had made cities, he had founded names. He had put gods in their shrines ...".*

(b)   Fragment of a Sumerian tablet (beginning of 2nd millennium), the story of the flood: *"...after the..... of kingship had been lowered from heaven.... he perfected the rites and exalted divine laws....founded the five cities in pure places, called their names, apportioned them as cult centers".*

(c) Babylonian cosmology (6th cent. B.C.) from Sippar (the god Marduk is the creator): *"The house he built, the city he built.... Nippur he built, Ekur he built, Uruk he built, Eanna he built....".*

(d) Genesis 11:4: "And it came to pass as they journeyed to the East that they found a plain in the land of Shinar and they dwelt there.... and they said, 'Come let us build us a city, and a tower at the top which may reach into heaven; and let us make ourselves a name, lest we be scattered upon the face of the whole earth...' ".

(see Paul Lampl, *'Cities and Planning in the ancient Near East'*, publ. STUDIO VISTA, London)

49 Epicurus, op.cit., p.218, 'Ουκ ην τι καθ'εαυτό δικαιοσύνη, αλλ' εν ταις μετ' αλλήλλων συστροφαίς καθ' οπηλίκους δήποτε αεί τόπους συνθήκη τις υπέρ του μη βλάπτειν ή βλάπτεσθαι. (There was never justice per se. It was always a convention, which was being accepted in different places through reciprocal associations of men and aimed at not hurting and not being hurt).

50 Amorson notes the ambiguity of the use of the work 'end': the town exists for the sake of this harmony, OR, the town ceases to have a raison d'etre once the harmony is achieved; to this he does not give an answer.

51 *"....all these [objects] show the same simple and very beautiful spiral curve. And all alike consist of stuff secreted or deposited by living cells, all grow, as an edifice grows; by accretion of accumulated material, and in all alike the parts once formed remain in being and are thenceforward incapable of change".* D' Arcy Thomson, *"On growth and form"*, Cambridge University Press, 1961, p. 175.

52 It coincides with successive positions of the radius vector.

53 Caspar Amorson seemed particularly amused and excited by this anarchic mode of town building, and its similarities with contemporary practice, and attempted a synthesis of the typical Aegean agglomeration by piecing together the scattered information given by Ladidlas. Caspar speaks of his work as 'a rigorous conceptualisation', but I do not think one requires a lot of imagination to restore the antiquity from the contemporary picture in this particular instance, where certain traditional elements tend to survive over

the centuries; I must admit though that his sketches based on hypotheses about the future merit some credit.

54   Caspar Amorson gives, in his comments, a classification of the two types of helix-towns using a contemporary vocabulary: *"Character of towns that developed from the centre outwards: individualistic and materialistic society, entrepreneurial and commercial mentality, weak central government but strong group bondages, classic and land value attraction of the city centre. Character of towns that reversed the direction of town expansion: idealism, strong social control, discipline and obedience in accomplishing planned collective long-term goals, self-denial in postponing satisfaction of material needs in favour of future generations. The society that produced the latter practiced a non-authoritarian, non-bureaucratic ideologically-motivated communism"*.

55   Ladislas in his coloured drawing wavers between Tesebaini, Arsashkun and Uhlu, all three mentioned in the Assyrian King Sargon II's account of his victorious war that put an end to Urartu's independence. I am more inclined to consider that the town was Uhlu, judging from this description: *"The city of Uhlu, a stronghold at the foot of Mount Kishpai...they did not drink, they did not satisfy their hunger...Ursa (Rusa I), their king...showed them where the water gushed forth, a ditch carrying these flowing waters, he dug, a...brought plenty like the Euphrates. He made numberless channels lead off from its bed...and irrigated orchards..."* (Paul Lampl, p. 48).

56   Caspar Amorson wonders, from our contemporary perspective, how Ladislas, although suspecting that the civilisation of Tlön had reached a technological level unthinkable for his Age's technical achievements, did not produce a more imaginative explanation about the mega-stucture (which Amorson of course attributes to the infrastructure of a railway system)

57   Amorson formulated a hypothesis that in some regions of extremely advanced technology –where decentralisation of energy production did not take place- human communities had attempted massive organised abandonment of the planet for space destinations. This he based on the frequent finding in subterranean edifices of engravings of a schematic bird-like form reminiscent of spacecrafts.

58   Amorson treats this subject, as the reader can already guess, with utmost seriousness, hypothesising that human societies had to protect their ecological environments from the calamities of a deranged climate and the enmity of nature during the Ecological Crisis Era. Amorson clearly dates the city planning of the Plateau of the Subterranean Ruins at the Second Period of the Era, when the Environmental Wars

were already in action, whereas he considers the cities and the city culture developed in the Plateau of the Helices as dating from Tlön's Golden Age.

59   Paul Lampl, p.113.

60   A stadium equals 202 yards

61   Which Caspar Amorson considers the infrastructure of a modern rail transportation system.

62   Names written in greek by Ladislas; it is not clear whether they were actually inscribed in greek or whether L. uses greek terminology out of a kind of erudite obligation.

63   In this section of Ladislas's text many terms appear in greek language. Περίπτερον: a building surrounded by a stoa on all sides.

WORKS CITED

Αβραμίδης, Γ. (2000), *Επίκουρος,* Αθήνα, ΘΥΡΑΘΕΝ. [Avramides, G. (2000), Epicurus, Athens, publ. THYRATHEN].

Amorson, Caspar (1998), *'A first reading of the Ladislas Manuscript',* Annual Review of Scandinavian Studies, Copenhagen.

__ (2001), *Addendum to 'the Ladislas Manuscript',* (Chapter *'Notes on the Architecture of Tlön'*).

Burckhardt, Titus (1970), *'The Heavenly Jerusalem and the Paradise of Vaikuntha',* Studies in Comparative Religion, Vol. 4/1Winter 1970, ©World Wisdom,Inc. www.studiesincomparativereligion.com

Borges, Jorge Luis (1965), *Fictions,* London, John Calder.

__ (1964), *Labyrinths,* N.Y., New Directions Books.

D' Arcy WentworthThomson, (1966), *On growth and form,* Cambridge, Cambridge University Press.

Dhammika, Ven. S. (1993), *The Edicts of King Ashoka –an English Rendering,* Kandy Sri Lanka, Buddhist Publication Society.

Ferguson, Nigel, (Sept.11,2006), *The Nation that fell to Earth,* TIME magazine.

Lampl, Paul (-), *Cities and Planning in the ancient Near East,* London, STUDIO VISTA.

Matthews, W.H., (1970), *Mazes and Labyrinths their history & development,* N.Y., Dover Publications.

Russell, Bertrand (1921), *The analysis of mind.*

Whitehead, Alfred N. (1964), *Science and the Modern World,* N.Y., Mentor Books.